Ms Blaelock's Book of Stress Free Dinner Parties

Also by Alexandria Blaelock

Ms Blaelock's Books
Stress Free Dinner Parties
Signature Wardrobe Planning
Holistic Personal Finance
Minimally Viable Housekeeping

Short Stories
Alma's Grace
Balancing the Book
Fate in Your Hands
Kiss of Death
Lady of the Looking Glass
Life in the Security Directorate
Long Weekend in the Snow
Love in the Security Directorate
Needy Bitch
Payton's Run
Phoenix Child
Shining Star
Ship in a Bottle
Simone Says Hands in the Air
The Guardian's Vigil
The Life and Death of Carmelita Basingstoke

Ms Blaelock's Book of Stress Free Dinner Parties

Alexandria Blaelock

BlueMere Books
MELBOURNE, AUSTRALIA

Copyright © Alexandria Blaelock, 2015, 2019.

Originally published as Stress Free Dinner Parties: How to plan, host and enjoy your party

All rights reserved. No part of this publication may be reproduced, distributed or transmitted in any form or by any means, including photocopying, recording, or other electronic or mechanical methods, without the prior written permission of the publisher, except in the case of brief quotations embodied in critical reviews and certain other non-commercial uses permitted by copyright law.

For permission requests, contact enquiries@bluemerebooks.com.

Ordering Information:
Discounts are available on quantity purchases. For details, contact orders@bluemerebooks.com

Stress Free Dinner Parties/Alexandria Blaelock.

hardback ISBN: 978-0-6481733-5-9
paperback ISBN: 978-0-6481733-6-6
digital ISBN: 978-0-6481733-7-3

Book Layout © 2015 BookDesignTemplates.com
Cover Image © RetroClipArt/Shutterstock.com

BlueMere Books
www.bluemerebooks.com

My heartfelt thanks go to my good friend Cindi, without whom this book would not exist.

Contents

Introduction	1
PART ONE: Plan Your Dinner Party	7
Budget	9
Guests	13
Theme	27
Food	31
Drinks	39
Other Needs	55
PART TWO: Prepare For Your Dinner Party	65
3 - 4 Weeks Before	67
1 - 2 Weeks Before	77
The Day Before	89
The Day	93
The Day After	105
APPENDIX A: Notes for Dinner Guests	107
APPENDIX B: What Alexandria Does	119
APPENDIX C: Our Italian Themed Dinner Party	123
Glossary	137
Bibliography	139
Index	141
Author's Note	144
About the Author	145

Introduction

HELLO! THANKS FOR BUYING MY book. I hope it helps you plan and host a Dinner Party that's talked about for decades - for all the right reasons.

Dinner Parties can be awesome get-togethers celebrating friendship, pleasure and beauty; they shouldn't be as horrifyingly stressful as trying to get into an Ivy League University. They should be an exciting and enjoyable puzzle.

And with good planning and preparation, you *can* relax and enjoy your guest's company from the moment they arrive.

Don't be fooled by the agony and ecstasy you see on reality television shows like *MasterChef* and *My Kitchen Rules*.

First of all, those shows aren't reality, and secondly Dinner Parties don't take place within those kinds of constraints.

They're as simple or as complicated as you want to make them. You can take as much or as little time as you like - 20 minutes to carefully plate up, or slap the food down in a millisecond or less.

You won't even have a chef judging the food. Unless of course you're friends with one and have invited them. But I'm inclined to think any chef would love it if you just made them scrambled eggs on toast, because *you* made it for *them*.

I can't imagine some of the celebrity chefs I've seen on television get invited to many people's homes to eat - Gordon Ramsay is unlikely to receive an invitation to eat in my home!

Aside from how grumpy he always seems, I don't think he'd like my simple style of cooking.

But take heart. Expectations about entertaining are in a constant state of change.

Before the nineteenth century, for example, Dinner Party service was *à la française* - the French or family style, in which all dishes are presented at the same time and guests help themselves. This is similar to the modern buffet and is a very practical approach when you've little in the way of furniture.

At the turn of the nineteenth-century, the Russian ambassador is reputed to have introduced a new style of service, *à la russe*, in which food is brought to the table in staged courses. Most modern restaurant and Dinner Party meals now proceed in this Russian style.

It's only a few decades since Dinner Parties were truly formal affairs, with dinner suits and bow ties. Not that those can't be fun too, but one does expect a stultifying degree of good manners and a separate dining room for that.

Mrs Beeton was entirely correct when she claimed "Dining is the privilege of civilisation."

In those days, it was the privilege of the wealthy; the hostess set the date and determined the distinguished guests, her Cook set the menu and prepared the food, and her Butler more or less coordinated everything else.

Stress Free Dinner Parties

The hostess received her guests safe in the knowledge her household machinery ensured all the arrangements were perfect, and she merely had to be charming.

In those Halcyon Dinner Party Days, dinners were always large and formal, contrasted with an "informal" little dinner for up to eight guests with whom you were intimate.

The manners were still formal but there was less ceremony, fewer courses and the best china was not used. The dress code would be lounge suits rather than white tie.

Modern life centres on simple, informal and integrated arrangements. Many of us don't have a separate kitchen, dining or living rooms - just one room, possibly delineated by tasteful area rugs.

One by one, the formal barriers between people have slipped away, and Dinner Party boundaries have moved a little to accommodate those changes too.

This book suggests an informal approach to Dinner Parties - assuming that's not an oxymoron of its own. It aims to maximise the time spent with your guests and minimise the time spent in the kitchen wrestling with food production.

This approach is helped by an open-plan layout; you can chat with your guests while you plate up, and maybe someone will transfer the plates from countertop to table.

I recommend you start by reading this book cover to cover to get a feeling for the contents, and then go over the overall planning and scheduling elements a second time.

We all have different upbringings and educations so some of it might need more thought than other bits.

Once you're comfortable with the overall process, you can start planning your own Dinner Party.

I describe the process as if one person is taking care of the whole event. It's much easier when you've someone to help, but you can host a fabulous Dinner Party alone if you limit your aspirations and plan it out very well.

Your meal service may consist of any number of courses, depending on your time and ingenuity. At the very least, you should consider five courses:

> *Apéritif:* pre-dinner drink with light snacks pending the arrival of all guests.
>
> **Appetiser:** a small first course at table.
>
> **Main:** a second, larger course with sides.
>
> **Dessert:** a small sweet course.
>
> *Digestif:* Coffee (or tea) with a fortified wine, liqueur or distillation, and a little sweet treat or chocolate.

You can reduce this by combining the *apéritif* and appetiser, or combine dessert with *Digestif*, or both.

Conversely, you could expand this by serving any number of individual dishes sequentially as many of the larger set meals do:

- Three appetiser courses (e.g., seafood, soup and salad).
- Three mains (e.g., fish, fowl [bird] and field [pasture animals like cows or sheep]).
- Three desserts (e.g., cream, frozen and fruit).

But for your own sanity, take Emily Post's advice and offer no more than eight courses including *apéritif* and *Digestif*!

While Mrs Beeton made some potential seasonal menu suggestions (both *à la française* and *à la russe*), they won't work for a solo host and don't suit modern tastes - Calf's Head, Tongue and Brains anyone?

Stress Free Dinner Parties

This book uses the example of a five-course dinner for six people. It draws against Marcella Hazan's "Sumptuous Summer Dinner" menu from her excellent cookbook, *Essentials of Classic Italian Cooking*. My versions of the recipes shown below are contained in *Appendix C: Our Italian Themed Dinner*.

Apéritif: ricotta and anchovy crostini with Prosecco, (optional Campari).

Appetiser: penne with roasted pepper sauce and Prosecco.

Main: pan-roasted veal and green bean salad with Pinot Grigio.

Dessert: mangoes and strawberries in sweet white wine with Moscato.

Digestif: coffee (or tea), amaretto and biscotti.

PART ONE:
Plan Your Dinner Party

THIS PART GIVES YOU THE key elements to consider when planning your Dinner Party. With this worked out, you'll have a clear picture of your meal, and avoid common entertaining pitfalls.

CHAPTER 1

Budget

It's hard to know what comes first - the theme, the menu or the budget.

As a one-time professional event manager, I can assure you it's the budget.

Your successful event management career depends on delivering the best possible event, on time and on or under budget.

And it's ridiculously easy for costs to escalate out of control if you don't keep on top of them.

A special celebratory meal should cost more than a simple meal to catch up with friends.

Your first wedding anniversary might cost $500, or your tenth $5,000, but regardless of the limit you set, you shouldn't need to take out a second mortgage to pay for it.

Your key components will, of course, be food and drinks; wine alone could cost $80 for a simple meal, but if the occasion is very special you might spend $250 or more.

Also, you might need to buy particular cooking and serving utensils, table linens, and even things like extra soap and toilet paper. You may also need to include the cost of furniture, professional cleaning and equipment hire.

It's worth setting a ballpark amount you can afford, then working through the costs to see what you can do with it.

Then you can make an informed decision about whether you need to increase your budget, or cut costs here and there to bring the total down.

Before you start planning, you'll already have an idea of whether your budget is ground, chuck, T-bone or fillet steak. And this knowledge will help you shape a Dinner Party you can afford.

I've included hints on reducing costs in the relevant sections where you might need them, rather than putting them here where you may need to come back to them.

When I'm managing a project, I give myself an objective - achieve some end at a particular cost by a specified date. For a Dinner Party, this would be something like:

> Host an Italian themed Dinner Party for six people for $500 on October 4 (St Francis' day, for the Patron Saint of Italy).

Then, if a time comes when I have to rethink my arrangements, I can decide which aspect is the most important and choose whether I need to change the theme, the number of guests, the budget or the date.

SUMMARY

Always set a budget first.
- Then see what you can do with it.
- Choose whether to increase your budget or cut your costs.

CHAPTER 2

Guests

DEPENDING ON WHO YOUR GUESTS are; Dinner Parties can be great fun. In fact, I think a good guest mix is more important than the food.

Watch almost any given period drama (Agatha Christie adaptations are always good for this), and there will almost inevitably be an excellent demonstration of "good" and "bad" guests; from the funny ones to the interminable bores.

For your Dinner Party, you need a balanced mix of talkers and listeners, smart people and those not so smart, all brought together in such a way they'll entertain each other.

And if your guests enjoy themselves, they'll think and say they had a great time no matter what the food was like.

Dietary Requirements

People's dietary needs can be a minefield. It's always a good idea to check with all your guests, even those you've fed before, because health needs change and many people prefer to keep it to themselves.

You may not have noticed "David" is a vegetarian who doesn't eat meat on religious grounds. You might know "Rebecca" is on a strict paleo diet (because she never stops talking about it), but you might not know "Shane" is allergic to shellfish or "Chelsea" is allergic to peanuts.

You might also like to find out whether guests with dietary requirements are sick of particular dishes.

There was a time I had to follow a reduced potassium diet and I reached the point I didn't want to eat mushroom risotto ever again, (still haven't).

The distinction between lifestyle choices and allergies is an important one.

"Rebecca" might claim she can't eat anything other than the foods our Palaeolithic ancestors ate, but she won't die if she does, whereas without prompt medical attention, "Shane" will if he takes the tiniest bit of shellfish.

"David" might eat eggs, but "Chelsea" absolutely cannot eat peanuts. Possibly other nuts as well.

You should also consider other food-related issues your guests might have. For example, false teeth wearers will prefer to avoid food with sharp edges that can get wedged underneath their dentures (e.g. nuts), tough, chewy foods like steak that might chafe or sticky food like peanut butter that could dislodge them.

Once you have this information, you can plan a menu that won't send your guests home hungry or ill, which is always the best outcome for a Dinner Party!

You might choose to serve an appetiser of vegetarian frittata with a spicy salsa instead of flash-fried prawns or chicken satay sticks.

Guest Numbers

The number of guests directly impacts your Dinner Party.

Aside from cost, you'll need enough covers (plates, cutlery, glasses and linens) for all and know whether you're prepared to buy or borrow more.

Plus the amount of intimacy you can manage and the amount of effort required. Fewer guests make a more intimate occasion and more guests increase the logistical challenges of the event.

In the Halcyon Days of Dinner Parties, the minimum number of guests was 10, to make a party of 12. But in those days, there was at the very least one maid to help out.

Two Couples (total party of four people)

Two couples make an intimate affair, best between people who know each other well. If you don't know each other well, the conversation may be stilted, or the close quarters can encourage over-sharing. If you're entertaining your boss and their partner, bear this in mind.

Three Couples (party of six)

Three couples is a good size for a more formal evening. It's a little less intimate than two and provides easy conversation access to the people seated across from and either side of you.

However, it's logistically more challenging than four. Generally, this is my preferred size.

Four Couples (party of eight)

Four couples can work, but the tendency is to form two conversational groups at each end of the table.

Even when your table is round.

And often someone from one end wants to join the action at the other end and there may be some furtive seat changing.

It's logistically challenging in the sense of space and resources required to seat and feed eight people at the same time.

Five couples (party of 10)

Five couples is almost unworkable for a sit-down dinner if you don't have some help.

They're more expensive, with a lot of food and drink and, of course, furniture and covers for 10.

You'll also need to spend more time managing people which might diminish your ability to enjoy the party.

I think this size group is where it starts getting easier to have a drinks party with some kind of snack service.

Six couples (party of 12)

Six couples is a lot of effort, but lots of fun when you've the right people, and immensely satisfying when it goes well.

To keep it manageable for one person to organise, focus on food you can cook slowly in bulk like casseroles, rather than fiddly quick cook single serve items like steamed fish parcels.

WHO TO INVITE

Halcyon Day Dinner Parties included an even number of men and women, on the assumption there'd be some discreet flirting and flattery between straight people.

They'd be married couples, a social set, and on occasion younger unmarried relatives mixed in. Seems quaint now doesn't it?

It's not so easy today, but at the same time, it's much easier because it doesn't really matter anymore.

Our modern lives are much less prescribed by social customs, and this has opened us up to a wider variety of experiences regarding religious, race, gender and sexuality mix.

A variety of different perspectives often makes for more fascinating dinner conversation.

People to Avoid

- People who're so judgemental it seems you'll never please them. You know who they are. Not only will they undermine your confidence in your arrangements, but they'll diminish the enjoyment of your other guests, and spoil your carefully crafted ambience.

- Those with such strong opinions they shut down all conversation around them with the totality of their opinions. Like the one person who thinks *Game of Thrones* is stupid when everyone else loves it.

- Those who won't stop arguing even though everyone either agrees or has surrendered. These often include fundamentalists, communists and, for some inexplicable reason, people who favour outlandish dietary guidelines. Unless of course your planned entertainment is extremist-baiting, in which case these people are perfect.

- Those with less careful grooming and manners. The ones who won't bathe between their afternoon sporting activities and your dinner, or will pick their noses in between courses.

- Anyone whom you know for certain is in the middle of a grudge match with one or more of your other guests.

People to Include

- The naturally hilarious - the ones who see the world slightly differently to "normal" people and can point out the difference.

- The clever and witty ones who come up with quick responses to cover conversational lulls.

- The sweet ones who say things like "That's fascinating, do tell me more."

- The curious ones (e.g., writers) who want to know more about everything.

Family

If you come from one of those families where everyone genuinely likes each other, and you all *really* want the best for each other, then you're truly blessed and can skip this section and move on to the next.

If you come from the kind of intensely competitive family, where members try to make themselves seem more impressive by downplaying the achievements of others, then read on.

Dinners with these kinds of families can be fraught with difficulty (if not danger).

> **Rivalry:** This is where you feel your meal needs to surpass the meal offered by whoever cooked last time. You might be tempted to try to make something very grand. But don't. This approach is a lot like casting pearls before the swine – they won't appreciate your effort unless it goes horribly wrong and they can torment you with it for the rest of your life.

> **Blood Feuds:** After a drink or two everyone relaxes a little, and you think it's going to be okay. But after another couple, someone refers to "the incident" and age-old feuds are resurrected along with the screaming and accusations. There's nothing you can do to stop this, it's a car wreck waiting to happen.

In both these cases, you need to lay some groundwork to prepare yourself for the meal.

1. Release any hope or expectation this time will be different.

2. Prepare your reliable menu (one you can rely on for consistently good results) so you can save your strength for dealing with the conversation.

3. Imagine ALL the things that could possibly go wrong, and how impossibly dire the end result could be (though a meteor hitting the house is very unlikely).

4. Make a note of things you can do something about, such as serving only two or three courses, allowing less time between courses, being very slow with the alcohol service and very quick with the water.

5. Pack away all your precious things - the ones you don't want to see mocked or broken.

Maybe this is an occasion when you'd prefer to spend more time in the kitchen, so learn how to make gravy from scratch.

While your roasted meat is resting, spoon most of the fat from the pan leaving the meat juices behind. Add enough flour to make a paste and put the pan on the stove over high heat. Gradually add a glass of wine and bring to the boil while whisking to make a smooth liquid. Add the water you used for steaming your vegetables and sufficient stock to make about 8.5 oz (250 ml) per person.

Grow herbs so you've the opportunity to leave the house to harvest some fresh herbs for your meal. Maybe you'd like to get a cheap frozen fruit pie and pre-packaged custard from the supermarket for a quick dessert.

Buy some really nice, really expensive Belgian chocolate to eat once everyone has left.

Make sure your schedule leaves you time to mentally prepare yourself before everyone arrives. Enjoy a moment or two of quiet stillness before the storm descends.

When things get hard, tell yourself this moment will pass, and then you can eat the chocolate and get back on track with the rest of your life. And while you eat the chocolate, be grateful a meteor didn't fall on your house.

Work Colleagues

At one time or other, you may have to entertain your boss, or you may want to entertain your work friends.

When it comes to entertaining your boss, you might want to show off, but don't. Prepare your reliable menu.

Do adequately cater the alcohol, but don't over indulge yourself. Any over sharing you or your partner do may affect your future prospects. Try to put yourself in a business meeting head space, and keep it as formal as possible.

When it comes to your work friends, (on the assumption you've invited them and their partners), try to talk about non-work things of interest to the whole table (not what "Rachel" the Personal Assistant said to you).

Bear in mind your conversation may drift into confidential territory and this could have employment consequences if the word gets out about something secret.

Again, don't show off; cook your reliable menu (your friends gossip about you too when you're not there).

Smokers

You probably know someone who smokes, even if you don't yourself. Or if you do, you'll know someone who doesn't.

For a Dinner Party, you need to decide how you're going to manage your smoker/non-smoker situation, particularly with the known hazards of passive smoking:

1. Not invite any smokers at all.

2. Ask them to smoke outside, and provide a place for them to do so.

3. Allow them to smoke at the table with or without arrangements for non-smokers.

4. Whether to treat e-smokers and tobacco smokers the same, (I recommend you do).

Matchmaking

If you want to do some matchmaking, I strongly encourage you not to. This sort of planned and managed event almost never leads to the production of a successful relationship. It's more likely to end the friendships.

No one likes to be set up without their knowledge or permission. The ill-fated lovers are bound to (rightly) question your judgement about the appropriateness of the match.

If matchmaking is your intention, leave it to "chance" and contrive an "accidental" meeting at a pub or cafe that's not pregnant with expectation.

WHAT TO TELL YOUR GUESTS

- The correct venue, date and time (I know I shouldn't have to say it, but it's happened before). Depending on your date and place, you might want to confirm the time zone – summer or winter, Eastern or Pacific, and so on.

- The availability of parking. Do they have to park on the street, or is there a lot nearby? If they have to pay for it, how much will it cost? Will they need cash or can they use a card?

- Pertinent theme details including dress code, whether children are included in the invitation, and any gift requirements (e.g. birthday).

- Whether alcohol will *not* be served when there might be a reasonable expectation it will be (and vice versa). And if it's a "dry" event, whether you'll allow guests to bring their own.

Getting Your Guests to Turn Up

I'm sorry to tell you the friends you've invited to your home might not arrive.

And worse, they might not tell you they won't be coming. I wish I could say they'll have a good excuse, but I can't. In about 98% of cases, it's just plain bad manners.

Treat it like a game and offer incentives, apply penalties and take a long-term approach:

Incentives

- Send a beautiful invitation card they can stick to the refrigerator and see every time they open the door.

- Invite someone they want to meet, and make sure they know the desired one is coming.

- Cook something you know they love to eat.

- Call or text them the week before with some inane question about the night, and let them know you're looking forward to seeing them.

- Post pictures of your preparations, and tag them on your social media channels, so they (and everyone they know) can see the effort you're making.

Penalties

- When the opportunity presents itself, gently chide your ignorant and inconsiderate friends by describing the meal and its once-in-a-lifetime, never-to-be-repeated perfection with great gusto.

- Occasionally refer to some hilarious joke or another thing they missed out on and then say "Oh that's right, you weren't there."

- Take Emily Post's advice and cut them from your list of potential dinner guests.

- If you hear someone else wants to invite them, you might mention they're unreliable; you invited them and they didn't arrive, nor did they offer apologies or excuses.

- Don't invite them to future events for a while. Talk about your upcoming events on social media to make sure they know what's planned and they aren't invited. (You might even get the fun of reminding them why this penalty has been applied).

Build Your Reputation

The absolute best way to have guests arrive is to build your reputation for hosting the BEST Dinner Parties. Learn to cook one or two dishes really well (your reliable menu), and become famous in your social set for bringing together the best company, the best food and generous drink service.

If your invitations are exclusive and highly sought after, people will seek you out and angle for invitations, so make sure your guests talk you up!

Be a Good Guest Yourself

If you're courteous, arrive on time, remember your party manners, and leave on time, people will be more inclined to do the same for you.

SUMMARY

The most important predictor of Dinner Party success are your guests. Aim for:

- An even number at table, and only invite as many as you can easily manage.

- A good balance of interesting and less interesting guests who will entertain each other.
- Don't forget to tell them when, where, and what.
- Use incentives and penalties to get them to turn up.

CHAPTER 3

Theme

ALL DINNER PARTIES NEED A theme to help narrow down your options.

As well as being a code to keep you focused on the time, cost and outcome, it brings together the food, table decorations, and to an extent your clothes, into a coherent event.

It doesn't have to be a theme in the sense of "Titanic", or "Murder on the Orient Express," though they're marvellous! It can be as simple as "Italian" or "Christian's Birthday".

A "French" theme will probably require more time and money than "Southern Barbeque". A fish and shellfish theme will take less time than chicken but cost more.

I suggest not having a Dinner Party with a "Housewarming" theme. These are better as very casual affairs with pizza or other catering.

Dinner Parties by their nature are intimate affairs, and it's best to be familiar with your new home's personality so it doesn't embarrass you.

If the toilet cistern takes a full 20 minutes to refill, you need to know before your guests do. Or if the taps make an unpleasantly loud noise while you wait for an inordinately long time for the hot water to come through.

Or if the chimney will draw the smoke from a roaring log fire. Whether the oven works, and so on.

Food

Once you've chosen your theme, a menu will often suggest itself. Your "Titanic" dinner implies period elements like oysters, fillet mignon and Waldorf pudding.

Correspondingly, "Christian's Birthday" might include his favourite dishes, or "Italian," yours.

DRINKS

Each of these themes in combination with the food implies matching drinks.

This might not be obvious, but none of the previously mentioned menus are likely to include Saki or Nam Bi Tua.

Different cultural dishes generally have accepted drinks to go with them. Sometimes regional specialities, such as a Chianti to balance the acidity of tomatoes or lassi to offset the spiciness of a curry.

Many regions also have traditional pre- and post-dinner drinks as well.

AMBIENCE

Your theme also suggests room and table decorations. "Titanic" might be starched white linen, silver and crystal (though to keep the cost down you might use paper, aluminium and glass).

"Christian's Birthday" might be balloons and streamers while "Italian" might be red, white and green and perhaps candles wedged in straw-wrapped Chianti bottles.

YOUR OUTFIT

I know there's an enormous temptation to rush out and buy a new outfit, and this is exactly the kind of thinking that quickly blows your budget. Particularly if it isn't well thought out.

Your theme may include requirements like period style, blood spatters for zombie outfits, green for St Patrick's Day or orange for Halloween. Aside from these, there are some other things you need to consider when you choose your outfit.

Cooking

You need to think about your menu, because ease of mixing, lifting, and bending matters. Ideally, your clothes will be loose enough to permit a good range of movement, but not so loose they drag in the food or get caught in your utensils.

You'll be in a hot kitchen and may need protection from hot oil and steam. You'll feel warmer because you'll also be moving around serving food and fetching drinks, and might not need a jacket or wrap until the *Digestif*.

This is an issue for shoes as well. If you're the kind of person who wears high heels all the time and has won prizes in high-heeled running races, then you're probably fine.

If you're not confident you can comfortably and elegantly cook and serve food in really high heels, then try a practice run or two; if it doesn't get easier, wear low heeled or flat shoes.

And a quick note about makeup. You'll probably be warm (and perhaps a little sweaty) and might not want to be dashing off to touch it up so a light application will be the most practical. You can, of course, test it out too.

I hope I don't need to mention clean fresh clothes?

Guests

Think about who's invited; for example, if "Abigail" is bringing her sleazy boyfriend you might want to wear something more modest than usual. Or if you're hosting an event for someone else, you might like to find out what they're wearing so you don't outshine them on the day.

Summary

Your theme guides your choice of:
- Food.
- Drinks.
- Decorations.
- The clothes you wear.

CHAPTER 4

Food

As I mentioned, your theme helps bring your party together, and to a large extent controls your menu.

And as you put together your menu, you'll probably identify areas where you can economise, as well as areas you may need a little more expenditure.

For example, to reduce costs, you could marinate your own olives. Rinse a jar of cheap olives in warm water, then gently heat in a pan with a good-quality olive oil, rosemary and garlic and leave to cool.

Or make your own crostini. Cut shapes from slices of an ordinary loaf of bread, brush with olive oil, sprinkle with salt and pepper and bake in a 350ºF (180ºC) oven until crisp. Cool before eating.

Other ways to reduce your costs are to shop at farmers' markets or ethnic grocery stores rather than supermarkets.

Asian stores are very good for bulk spices. (Don't be afraid to ask questions about the weird stuff you see - who knows what you might discover).

You can also maximise the use of rice, pasta and seasonal vegetables.

Or you might choose potluck and invite your guests to bring food or drinks. Though you should probably nominate each guest to bring something in particular or you risk several jelly courses (e.g. red, green and yellow).

If you like to stay in control, you might prefer to avoid this approach.

However, menu planning (and cost control) needs to take other things into account as well.

Dietary Requirements

The dietary needs of your guests must be taken seriously. If they CANNOT eat certain things (or are allergic), like nuts, gluten or dairy, you must NOT feed them these things as there will be serious health consequences for them.

Dietary preferences, like veganism, on the other hand, are not life-and-death considerations, but it would be kind of you to discuss them with your guests.

The Season

You'll probably not look forward to a substantial hot meaty dish like Boeuf Bourguignon in midsummer, nor will you want a light tuna niçoise in winter. However, something like a rack of lamb can form the basis of a good meal in summer or winter, depending on the cooking method and the side dishes you provide (e.g. salad or roasted vegetables).

Balance

The menu as a whole should balance:
- Rich with simple (e.g. four cheese tart followed by plain roasted chicken).
- Highly spiced with bland (Mexican chicken with rice)
- Light with dense (steak and salad).
- Snacks with substance (canapés and casserole).

You should also try to balance protein, carbohydrates and fat so the whole meal is not over heavy in one of these groups.

A simple way to do this is base each course on one group, for example, a light clear soup, followed by roasted meat with vegetables and a fruit salad. Instead of creamy soup, roasted meat with vegetables and a lemon meringue pie.

Or a light salad, meat and vegetable casserole and an apple pie with custard, cream or ice cream, rather than baked lentils, meat and vegetable casserole and a steamed suet pudding.

Cooking Method

It can be hard to manage the cooking if all the dishes use the same method, for example, require the oven at the same time. It's easier to deliver the hot food hot, and the cold food cold if each course uses a different method of preparation.

It's also a good place to control costs.

For example, most meat is muscle, and the muscles that move the most result in the toughest meat. Generally, the tougher the meat, the cheaper it is, and the more it benefits from long slow cooking to loosen tight muscle fibres.

This makes a stew or casserole one of the most economical dinners you can make.

It's worth noting these dishes also make the sort of luxurious meal people order at restaurants because they don't have the time to prepare them at home.

You can reduce your costs still further by substituting vegetables for some of the meat and serving with crusty bread.

Number of Courses

As mentioned in the introduction, you should offer a minimum of five courses:

1. *Apéritif:* pre-dinner drink with light snacks pending arrival of all guests.

2. Appetiser: a small first course at table.

3. Main: a second, larger (main) course with sides.

4. Dessert: a little sweet course.

5. *Digestif:* coffee (or tea) with an alcohol and sweet biscuits (cookies), tiny cakes (petit fours or mignardises) or chocolates.

In the Halcyon Days, the cheese was an additional compulsory course served before dessert, but these days it's customary to serve after.

If you want to cut costs, you could combine your *apéritif* and first-course food and drinks, or dessert *and* cheese, or dessert and cheese with *Digestif*. Or a combination of all.

Serving Sizes

Recipes usually suggest a range of serves, say four to six.

Unless you're using a planned menu, these suggestions are commonly made on the assumption one serving is either a meal on its own or perhaps one of two courses.

Five courses plus cheese and *Digestif* is a lot of food, so you should scale the courses, serves, or both down.

Overall, the three central courses should provide about 25.5 oz (700 g) of food; with about 17.5 oz (500 g) from the main and sides.

Apéritif

The *apéritif* is just a little something to do with your non-drinking hand, kind of like a tiny welcome gift. A small bowl of chips or nuts is usually sufficient, but you could up the ante with some crudités and dip, olives, or little things on crackers.

Appetiser

The first course is a little temptation, intended to get the digestive juices flowing. They're usually intensely flavoured, something like 1 oz (30 g) of pâté with a slice or two of crisp buttered toast, a stuffed tomato, two or three mushrooms, or 2.5 oz (70 g) of prawn cocktail per person.

Main

The main course is the largest part of the meal. Generally, it consists of 8 oz (225 g) of a meat dish, accompanied by two or three 3 oz (85 g) vegetable dishes per person.

Dessert

Dessert would be one cup of pudding, a slice of pie or cake with sauce to 8 oz (225 g) per person.

Cheese

Depending on your guests and circumstances, you might offer cheese instead of, or in addition to, a dessert.

If you do offer cheese, the usual arrangement is one hard (or old), one soft (young) and one blue.

These are served with crackers, crisp fruit like a green apple, dried fruit (a bunch of dried grapes looks spectacular), nuts and a fruit paste such as fig.

You need around 3 - 5 oz (85 - 140 g) of cheese per person.

If you can't afford this sort of platter, it's better to have one good-sized chunk of a superb cheese than ordinary ones.

Cheese is generally best at room temperature, served on a natural surface (wood or stone).

The cheese should be spaced widely across the board, each with its own knife to prevent the flavours mixing.

Some people like to lay them out in order of strength, but I just try to make it look nice.

You could label them if you want to, or if there's something particularly special about them.

Digestif

For *Digestif*, you should generally allow two or three little cakes for each guest. Or more if you've some sweet-toothed friends in the group.

CAN'T COOK/WON'T COOK/JUST STARTING OUT

Don't panic - you can still host a Dinner Party!

Take heart, start small, and keep practising. My friend Toseland's first Hollandaise Sauce was almost toxic, but now he can whip it up in a few minutes while blanching asparagus and poaching eggs for a quick lunch!

With one well-practiced and reliable meal, you can churn it out with minor variations for different guests. As you gain experience and become more confident, you can expand your reliable menu to include other dishes.

In the meantime, the quickest and easiest Dinner Party is going to be one where the least effort is required. For example:

> *Apéritif:* Champagne with potato chips (crisps) and nuts, or a jar of olives or other preserved vegetables.
>
> **Appetiser:** wrap a slice of honeydew or rock melon (canteloupe) in prosciutto with more Champagne. Grind a little pepper over the top and drip some good-quality olive oil on the plate to make it look fancy.
>
> **Main:** The kind of casserole where you throw 1" (2.5 cm) lumps of red meat and vegetables into a dish with stock (or a suitable wine) and cook in the oven for hours. Serve with red wine, bread rolls and a bag of dressed salad leaf.
>
> Make your own dressing by whisking together 3 tablespoons of olive oil with 1 tablespoon of white wine vinegar, one teaspoon of Dijon mustard, one clove of crushed garlic (or a teaspoon of garlic powder) and a little salt and pepper until it goes thick

and opaque. Make sure you guests can see you doing it; they'll think you're amazing.

Dessert: fruit or custard tart from a good bakery with ice cream or Chantilly Cream (full fat cream whipped with vanilla paste and icing sugar - start with one teaspoon of vanilla and one tablespoon of sugar and adjust the amounts of each until you really like it) served with a sweet wine.

Digestif: fancy "homemade" style shop bought biscuits/cookies with liqueur.

Don't attempt to produce dishes beyond your capability. Practice, practice, practice until they become second nature before you release them on unsuspecting guests.

Don't be ashamed to serve the same dish time and again - make it your reliable menu - it's better to serve something reliably delicious than not.

If you need an excuse tell your guests it's your favourite, or invite someone you know who likes the dish and say you made it for them.

And if your skills don't extend to dinner, consider a brunch, lunch or supper party instead (adjust your drinks and table decorations accordingly).

Failing that, buy something pre-prepared at the supermarket or order take-out and keep it warm until your guests arrive, before serving it on plates with cutlery.

Summary

A good meal is all about the balance.
- Make sure all dietary requirements are met.
- Prioritise fresh seasonal ingredients, and cook according to the weather.
- Balance the ingredients, the courses, and the amount of food.

CHAPTER 5

Drinks

Besides your theme, other things to consider include:

Dietary Requirements

Some red wines contain sulphites, such as sulphur dioxide, as a preservative, antioxidant and antibacterial agent.

It's not a problem for most people, but asthmatics and people who don't produce the particular enzyme required to break it down may have difficulties.

Those with these conditions will usually know, and if it's likely to be a problem, they'll be able to tell you. If no one mentions it, you can proceed with confidence as the use of sulphites is strictly regulated.

Additionally, if someone is allergic to nuts, you should avoid nut-based alcohols.

Food and Drink Matching

Drinks are usually matched to food courses.

If your recipe doesn't suggest anything and you aren't sure, do an internet search for "what wine matches..." and you'll find lots of suggestions.

Don't forget to try them before you commit yourself.

Let's look at our five courses again in further detail:

Apéritif

Generally, a small snack with one drink to whet your guest's appetite while you wait for everyone to arrive.

Your choice of drink will to an extent be determined by whether you're hosting with someone else or alone.

If you're going solo, you might prefer to restrict the drinks to something simple like Champagne, Sherry or Campari, but if there's someone to make them, offer cocktails if you prefer.

Appetiser

This heralds the start of the meal proper.

While your guests will only take one or two small glasses of this, it should match the course in lightness and texture.

For example, a light salad can be balanced with a light white wine such as Sauvignon Blanc. Or you might like a dry apple cider with a savoury slice of pork terrine.

Main

The main part of the meal. Your guests will drink two to four glasses, and as this course is usually substantial, you need a robust wine to balance it.

The old red wine with red meat and white wine with white meat is still a good rule of thumb, but spend some time reading the bottle labels as they often include suggestions about how to pair them.

Not to mention the same kind of wine can taste a little different depending on what you serve it with.

> **Beef:** a full-bodied red like Cabernet Sauvignon. Or for veal, a lush red like Merlot.
>
> **Lamb:** almost anything depending on the dish. Try a Merlot or Shiraz, or perhaps Chianti for Italian, Rioja with Spanish or Bordeaux for French.
>
> **Pork:** can be hard to match as it's often prepared with spices that don't sit well with wine. Try a dry Riesling or Rosé, Merlot, Pinot Noir or Shiraz.
>
> **Chicken:** a light white like Sauvignon Blanc, or for savoury, something richer like Beaujolais or Shiraz.
>
> **Turkey:** something light like Zinfandel for the traditional trimmings, or heavier like Chardonnay if not.

Duck: a mid-range red or white like Merlot, Chianti, Syrah or Chardonnay.

Goose: a rich Burgundy, or if served with sweet sides, then Riesling. Or maybe Pinot Noir or Shiraz.

Fish is a little more difficult as there's a large variety of fish available.

Meaty: fish like salmon or swordfish need something strongly flavoured like an oaked Chardonnay.

Strongly flavoured salty: like sardines or mackerel need something light and dry like Riesling or Rosé.

Medium: for hake or snapper, something not too sweet and not too dry like a Sauvignon Blanc.

Mild white: like sole or haddock, a light and refreshing wine such as Chablis or more Champagne.

Game is traditionally meat from wild animals, though more recently these are often farmed livestock as well.

Birds: such as duck, quail, pheasant, partridge, grouse and woodcock are good with mellow reds like Bordeaux, Rioja, Cabernet Shiraz, Syrah or maybe Chianti.

Venison: a really deep and complex red like Bordeaux or Cabernet Sauvignon.

Rabbit: a light red like Chianti, Burgundy or Beaujolais. Or perhaps a white like Pinot Gris or Sauvignon Blanc.

Dessert

Usually paired with a small glass of a sweet dessert wine like Sauternes, Moscato, or Riesling. In some cases, you might prefer something with a drier flavour such as a sparkling Rosé or stronger such as port to balance your dessert.

Cheese

Cheese can be tricky to match because they're all different; but generally red wine with aged cheese, sweet wine with salty, and dry with the soft, creamy ones.

Though by this stage of the evening, no one will care much about which wine is a good match with which cheese - they'll be drinking up all the leftovers from the other courses.

Digestif

Served with a post dinner coffee (or tea or both), this can be a fortified wine like Vermouth or port, liqueurs like Drambuie or Grand Marnier, or distillations such as Ouzo. You could also offer cocktails depending on who is helping you with drink service, and how soon you want people to leave.

HOW MANY DRINKS DO YOU NEED?

There are two methods of catering for drinks; by the bottle or in bulk.

By the Bottle

For catering purposes, one 750 ml bottle yields:

- 2 - 3 glasses of water
- 2 - 3 glasses of beer
- 5 glasses of wine
- 6 glasses of Champagne
- 16 shots of liquor/spirit

If we work on the assumption you've a total party size of six people, and you've invited them to arrive 6:30 for 7:00 then you'll require the following as a minimum:

- 2 bottles of Champagne for *apéritif*
- 2 bottles of wine for the first course
- 2 bottles of wine for the main course
- 2 bottles of wine for dessert
- 2 bottles of port or one spirit for *Digestif*

It's better to have too much wine than not enough, and while I'm told you can return unopened bottles of alcohol, it's rare I've found myself with an unopened bottle I could return.

Just to be sure, consider adding an extra bottle for each of the first three courses.

If you've guests who prefer beer to wine, then swap out glass for glass of wine with beer.

It's easier to manage beer delivery in smaller "single serve" bottles (swap one glass of wine for one bottle of beer).

You could also offer beer in addition to Champagne as an *apéritif*.

In Bulk

Alternatively, if you don't plan to provide a range of beverages throughout the night, you can cater by volume.

A person who is not troubled by thoughts of getting home is capable of drinking two drinks the first hour, but will generally slow down to one for each of the following hours - a total of 6 drinks over the evening.

Six people drinking six drinks will take 36 drinks from eight bottles of wine. Or one beer drinker six single serve bottles.

Or you could allow a 60/40 wine/beer split.

Most people have a preference for red or white wine, so technically you'd need a 40/40/40 split. But it's unlikely your dinner guests will complain so there's no need to stress too much about this.

Water and Soft Options

As people drink less alcohol as the evening progresses, they'll want more non-alcoholic (or soft) options to compensate.

As a minimum, you should allow one soft glass per person for each of the five hours (a total of 30 for six people) requiring 10 to 25 bottles of water.

I'm not sure I've ever done 25 bottles, but I've certainly used more than a dozen.

If you want to reduce your costs, use tap water in a jug, perhaps with some lemon slices or twists of peel for prettiness.

You must always have soft options available.

Some of them will be driving home and you cannot in good conscience permit them to do so if they have drunk a substantial amount of alcohol.

Others may not be drinking alcohol at all, so you might want to offer flavoured carbonated beverages, juices, or the like, and cater one to two quarts (litres) per three guests.

Ice

Ice at a Dinner Party can serve two functions; in glasses to chill individual drinks and in buckets to keep bottles cool.

You won't need much drinking ice for a wine-based Dinner Party, but the following helps with soft drinks and cocktails.

One pound (450 g) of ice per person per hour, is sufficient for both purposes. Our five hour six-person Dinner Party would require 30 lbs (13.6 kg).

If you've other arrangements for cooling the bottles, for example, a drinks fridge, you could cut this total to around 10 oz (285 g) per person per hour.

After three hours your guests will have finished the bulk of their eating and drinking so you may be able to skip the ice for the last couple of hours.

Bear in mind the weight of your container *and* ice *and* drinks puts you into the dangerous range of lifting.

If you want to avoid injuring your back, you'll need the help of another person to lift the container.

In Australia, it's common to use your laundry or utility sink which generally holds something like 47.5 qt (45 l), and can easily be emptied at the end of the night. If this is not an option for you, consider splitting the drinks between containers.

NOTES ON GLASSES AND POURING

Alcoholic beverages are generally served in different shapes and sizes of glasses, to enhance your drinking experience.

Crystal looks pretty and sparkly, requires special care, but doesn't provide a significantly better drinking experience than ordinary glass.

Glass is generally more durable than crystal - I use glass because I can put it in the dishwasher at the end of the party.

You don't need to buy a different glass for every kind of drink, you can manage with just two; red wine and tulip shaped Champagne glasses (or slender white wine glasses).

When you hold your glass by the bowl, you increase the temperature and movement of the wine inside it, so the best drinking experience is achieved by holding the stem.

The polite way to pour *apéritifs* or the first drink at the table is to start with the oldest woman through to youngest, then oldest to youngest man and finally yourself.

To save yourself from dizziness, travel the table in one direction (for the superstitious, clockwise).

Do be kind and offer the last sip to others, and only take it if everyone else declines.

For your Dinner Party, only pour the glass about half to two-thirds full, depending on the glass size.

Partly because it looks prettier this way, partly because domestic glasses aren't marked with standard measures, and partly because it's also an easy way to control the number (and cost) of drinks.

If you open each bottle as you go, you're less likely to have half-empty bottles at the end of the night. Open them in the kitchen rather than at the table, because things get messier as the evening progresses.

Champagne

For best results, Champagne should be served cool, not chilled.

The flavour is determined by the perfume of the gas escaping the bubbles when they hit the surface of the wine, so for optimum bubble movement, it should be served around 45ºF (7.5ºC). Champagne coupes (mythically modelled after an assortment of French Lady's breasts) allow the gas too much movement while some flutes allow it too little, so something tulip shaped is perfect.

To open the bottle, rip off the foil and loosen but don't remove the wire cage (safety first). Grasp the cork tightly and twist the bottle from its base. Pour it gently down the side of the glass to minimise the loss of bubbles.

White Wine

Whites are generally best at refrigerator temperature in the range of 44 - 57ºF (7 - 17ºC). Lighter wines, such as Sauvignon Blanc are better colder, and something heavier like an oaked Chardonnay is better warmer.

Generally, the lighter wines are served in a V-shaped glass to allow savouring of the aroma while Chardonnay bowls are U-shaped for greater exposure to flavour-enhancing oxygen.

Red Wine

The rich red wines that we generally think of when we say red wine (like Merlot and Cabernet Sauvignon) are best served at room temperature, in the region of 63 - 69°F (17 - 21°C), whereas the lighter reds like Rosés can be chilled like whites.

As with whites, the lighter fruitier wines are best in thinner tapered glasses and the heavier in wider bowls. If in doubt, go with a big round bowl!

Rich red wines often benefit from being "decanted".

This is when you pour wine into a decanter, which exposes the wine to oxygen and significantly improves the flavour.

Pour it down the side of the decanter to get the maximum air, and leave the last little bit in the bottle in case there are small bits of grape and twig in it (or pour it through a tea strainer).

Swirl the decanter a couple of times to mix the air in and leave for at least five minutes before drinking. Or buy an aerator and wedge it in the bottle neck before pouring into glasses.

Dessert and Fortified Wines

Dessert wines like Port and Sherry are generally served in small glasses, to intensify the flavour and minimise alcohol vapours (also excellent for liqueurs).

However, brandy should be served in a "snifter" which is warmed in the hands to release the aroma.

I recommend ignoring brandy until you've got a house well set up with other more useful things, because while brandy snifters make lovely dessert bowls, they're more or less single-purpose glasses.

Beer

These days you can buy an incredible array of beers, and aficionados will tell you that just like wine they have recommended glasses and serving temperatures as well, in the range of 36 - 59°F (2 - 15°C). I'm going to go out on a limb and say from the refrigerator is fine.

In general, strong beers come in smaller glasses.

Toseland tells me beer company glasses are shaped to highlight the pretty bits, for example, his favourite wheat beer comes in a glass that's tall and thin to show off its colour.

Others come in tulip-shaped glasses with stems to emphasise the aroma. If in doubt go with the tulip shaped for the same reasons as wine - to stop your hands changing the temperature and movement of the beverage.

Beer is best poured down the side of the glass to minimise froth formation.

Spirits

You can also get an incredible array of spirit glasses. Depending on how you plan to mix them, you can manage with just large and small tumblers (which can also be used for water).

A "shot" of spirit varies from country to country, somewhere in the region of 0.8 - 1.5 oz (25 - 45 ml).

They come in single serves or doubles (twice as much as a single) and some countries also offer smalls (half a single).

I wouldn't generally recommend more than one shot for Dinner Parties, and only as a pre-dinner cocktail.

Drinking and Driving

As a responsible host, you should take into account the amount of alcohol your guests can drink and still legally drive (as opposed to safely).

It gets a little tricky here, as there's no international agreement on how much alcohol is in a standard drink, what the maximum permitted volume of alcohol in the blood is, or how many standard drinks you can have without exceeding the maximum blood alcohol content.

Fortunately, scientists agree on the calculations, so here's the process for working it all out.

Standard Drinks and Alcohol Units

A "standard" drink is the amount of an alcoholic beverage that contains a given volume of *pure* alcohol. The levels are set by legislation and depending on where you live you might see these expressed as drinks by volume in millilitres or units of mass in grams.

Unfortunately, there isn't a nice neat 1:1 ratio between standard drinks and alcohol units, so depending where you're hosting your Dinner Party, you may need to calculate them.

The easiest way to calculate the number of standard drinks by volume is:

volume (in millilitres) x % of alcohol by volume ÷ volume of standard drink

for example, 375 ml of full-strength beer (5% alcohol by volume)

= 375 x 5% ÷ standard drink = (see results over the page)

Or to calculate the number of standard units by weight (in the UK), the formula is:

volume (in millilitres) x % of alcohol by volume ÷ 1000

for example, 375 ml of full-strength beer (5% alcohol by volume)

= 375 x 5 ÷ 1000 = 1.875 units

Here is a small comparison of the standard drinks and alcohol units in different countries. It was correct at the time of writing, but the law changes more often than you might think, so don't rely on this and check the local laws to be certain.

	Iceland and the United Kingdom	Australia, France, Ireland, New Zealand, and Spain	Portugal and the United States of America	Japan
Mass (g)	8	10	14	19.75
Volume (ml)	10	12.7	17.7	25
# drinks	1.875	1.476	1.06	0.75
# units	1.875	1.87	1.88	1.88

Table 1: Comparison of Pure Alcohol in "Standard" Drinks

Fortunately for Australian drinkers, this information is on the label. If you don't live in Australia, check your label just in case (and let me know). For comparison, these are one standard Australian drink:

- 16 oz (475 ml) light beer
- 8.5 oz (250 ml) full-strength beer
- 3.8 oz (111 ml) white wine

- 3.6 oz (107 ml) Champagne
- 3.4 oz (100 ml) red wine
- 2.4 oz (75 ml) port
- 1 oz (30 ml) gin

Blood Alcohol Content

In general, any level of alcohol in the blood will impair a person's judgement, so most countries apply a maximum blood alcohol (BAC) limit.

Again, there's no international consensus on what that is, or whether it's measured by volume (as grams of alcohol per 100 millilitres of blood) or mass (as grams of alcohol per 100 grams of blood).

However, it's usually expressed as a percentage of *pure* alcohol in the given volume or mass of blood.

Permitted levels range from nil to 0.1%, and you should learn the requirements of your jurisdiction.

While it's expressed as a measurement of blood, most countries take their initial measurements with a breathalyser unless there's a particular need for blood to be taken.

Where a driver is detected with a BAC that's higher than the legal level, they face penalties including fines, loss of licence and perhaps imprisonment.

Always assuming they don't crash and kill or injure themselves or someone else first, which is a whole other mess of trouble.

While every drinker is different, the scientific community mostly agrees one standard drink could increase your blood alcohol concentration to 0.02% as quickly as half an hour after you drink it, but take as long as two hours for the liver to break it down.

Where possible, encourage your guests not to drink and drive, and make provision for emergency sleepovers.

If you're not confident a guest can *safely* drive (legally or not), consider taking their car keys and calling them a taxi.

Summary

A good meal is all about the balance.
- Take dietary requirements into account.
- Match drinks to the dishes
- Consider buying in bulk or by the bottle.
- Ensure you have plenty of non-alcoholic options.
- Use ice to chill bottles and individual drinks.
- Use the right glasses for the right drinks.
- Consider your guest's ability to drive home safely.

CHAPTER 6

Other Needs

NOW YOU KNOW HOW MANY people to cater for and what the menu is, so you know how much food and drink to buy.

The next thing is to start looking at what else you need. This is a mix of practicality and ambience.

Practicalities

Let's start with the basics.

Ummm... You!

Well, your most charming, courteous, friendly and gracious self anyway. None of those less perfect versions of you thank you very much!

While you're engrossed in conversation, you'll still be paying attention to what's going on around you in case there's a situation that needs attending to, for example, replacing glasses, cutlery or napkins as required.

If the conversation lags, you might invite "Adam" to relate a clean yet amusing anecdote he told you earlier, or start a story about when you and "Cassandra" did something and ask her to finish it.

You know which of your guests will rise to this challenge.

You may at times need to draw attention to someone who's excluded from the conversation by both neighbours and you may be as blunt as you wish.

Halcyon Day hostesses were advised to suggest to female guests that they may not monopolise Mr So-and-So any longer because Mr Such-and-Such was trying to attract her attention.

I'm not sure that approach would work quite as well in modern times, but knowing your guests, you should be able to think of some way to chastise the neighbours.

Though if you keep your numbers on the lower side of the spectrum this is unlikely to be an issue.

Furniture

You'll need some! At the very least something for each person to sit on while eating.

The general decorating consensus is that a dining table should fit the following dimensions:

4 – 6 people	4' (122 cm) circular/square table
	2'6" x 5' (76 x 152.5 cm) oval/rectangle
6 - 8 people	5' (152.5 cm) circular/square table
	3' x 6' (92 x 183 cm) oval/rectangle
8 - 10 people	6' (183 cm) circular/square table
	3'6' x 8' (107 x 244 cm) oval/rectangle

There should be about 24" (61 cm) between seats, and about 36" (91.5 cm) between the table and nearby walls or non-dining furniture.

The amount of space available to you is the determining factor in your choice of dining furniture - there's no point having furniture that takes up so much space that you can't use it or so little that your guests feel dwarfed by the space.

Tiny home dwellers need to be creative.

If you're planning to buy something, look for a table that has "leaves" that expand seating capacity. Some can be removed from the table and stored separately, others fold into the table.

If you aren't buying furniture, and you don't have another table you can use, you could build your theme around it.

Move all the excess furniture and knickknacks into another room, then:

- arrange the furniture like a train dining car.

- throw a rug on the floor and call it a picnic.
- lay cushions on the floor and go Japanese.
- hang some draperies and go on a South African Safari.

If you've larger accommodations, you might also want a more comfortable second space for receiving guests and enjoying your *apéritifs* and *Digestifs*.

Covers

You'll need a cover for each guest. Having one or two spares is also useful for breakages and other mishaps.

Serving ware

You need to think about how your food is going to be served:

- Do you want big platters so people can serve themselves, or will you plate individually?
- Are you serving both appetisers and desserts on small plates or in bowls? Could you serve one of the courses in a similar but different kind of container, like a teacup or saucer?
- Will you have enough glasses for each of your guests to use two or three as the night progresses? Can you make any substitutions, such as small tumblers or glass cups for the *apéritifs* or *Digestifs*?
- Will you have enough knives, forks and spoons? Can you replace them with something similar, such as teaspoons for dessert spoons?

Cooking Utensils

Read through your recipes to see what you need. Some cookbooks are very helpful and will tell you exactly what you need, but with others you'll need to work it out for yourself:

- If you need one teaspoon of something, then you need a set of measuring spoons.

- If you need half a cup of something, you need a set of measuring cups.

- If you need to slice, dice or chop something, you need a sharp knife and a chopping board.

    You should have one knife and one board for meat, and one for vegetables, but if you only have one make sure you wash it well when you swap from meat to vegetables, to avoid bacterial cross contamination.

- You might be able to minimise the number of pots and pans that you need by washing them out between courses, but you should think about whether you want to do that while your guests are watching you.

- Make a note of the utensils you don't have. When you've got your full list together, see if there's anything that you already have that you can use instead. For example, if you've a measuring jug, you might not need measuring cups for liquids.

Your proposed menu may use tools and utensils that you don't own. A Spanish menu may require a paella pan and this requires a choice between using your existing fry or sauté pan or buying something.

I recommend that if you need to manage the cost, your sauté pan will do as you can't use a paella pan for much other than paella. Or you could make cocido (a kind of stew) instead.

Having said that, if you find you really like paella, and think you might eat it a lot in the next few decades, then it's worth buying the best quality pan you can afford.

Much better than buying first and leaving it unused in the cupboard for the same period of time.

You can often buy bulk quantities of utensils and serving ware from restaurant supply stores, big box stores and discount department stores.

Purchasing this way is also useful for replenishing breakages over time without having to invest in a full new service. Or if you don't feel it's essential for it all to match, visit your local charity or thrift store.

Apron

And on the subject of cooking, at some point, you'll need something to protect your fancy clothes from cooking splashes.

A "full-length" apron that covers a substantial portion of your top as well as your bottom is best; you'd be amazed which bits of you get splattered with fat.

Home Comforts

Then there are little things that make for a lovely evening, like:

- An overwhelming abundance of toilet paper.
- Sufficient towelling that your guests will not be drying their hands on wet towels.

AMBIENCE

Ambience is the mood or atmosphere you want to create. Just consider for a moment the difference between a family meal and one you might make for your lover.

Good bright lighting against soft and romantic. Solid functional serving ware versus refined and delicate. Robust and filling dishes versus tiny titbits to feed by hand.

As you can see, there's quite a difference...

So coming back to your Dinner Party. You've:

- Chosen a date which might have special lighting and decoration requirements - think Easter versus Halloween.

- Picked a theme such as "Italian."

- Invited guests, some of whom might have particular requirements, for example, elderly guests may prefer not to sit in a draughty high traffic location.

- Worked out a menu. If you're making food with an extreme splash risk, say fettuccine in tomato sauce, you might prefer bright lighting so guests can see what they're doing. Foods with a lesser spill risk, say sliced meat with vegetables, could manage with dimmer lighting. Or maybe you could offer your lobster eaters bibs. I recommend offering foods with minimal splash risk - I don't want to put my friend Katy's dry cleaner's kids through university, or hear that they couldn't save her favourite silk blouse.

Linens

Each guest should have their own napkin. You might like a few spares as well in case guests use them to mop up spills.

You might like to add a table cloth; their original purpose was to protect the furniture though more recently they have become decoration if not disguise. You can dress a classic white up or down for any occasion, as long as it's made from a thick and durable fabric and in good repair.

Centrepieces

If your table is big enough, a centrepiece can look pretty. It should match your table's; not too large and not too small.

However, if your table is comparatively large, you'll need a condiment set for each side of it.

Appropriate centrepieces are bowls piled high with fruit or floral arrangements. Or, depending on the season and theme, an interestingly shaped branch from the garden.

Fruit can be inexpensive as well as attractive, with the added bonus of being edible over the days following dinner.

However, for a Dinner Party, they're a decoration that must be carefully arranged to provide a feast for the eyes, not just bunged in the bowl anyhow.

If you choose flowers, use unscented ones that won't compete with the aromas of the meal. If you use lilies or other flowers with pollen-laden stamens, snip the stamens short to remove the pollen; yellow pollen stains are almost impossible to remove and your guests won't thank you for that.

If you know that some of your guests have asthma, allergies or hay fever, go to a professional florist and ask for recommendations about the most appropriate arrangement for your area.

Branches can look spectacular, but you'll need to brush them down to remove bugs and dust. Try to pick a species that's not going to leak sap.

Alternatively, many florists and craft shops stock twigs which have already been cleaned up and bleached or dyed; these would serve the same purpose, or could perhaps be arranged in a vase as if they were flowers.

Candles

Candles can be lovely, providing they're placed to provide adequate light for eating - ideally between each guest.

They should go in the centre of the table so they don't set your guest's hair on fire, but not so central that they set your decorations on fire either.

The sticks should also be short or tall enough that the candle flame is not at eye level, and your guests can see around it to talk without getting flame glare.

The candles themselves should be in proportion to the sticks (or holders) - thin candles with slender sticks and fat candles with thick sticks. The candles should be unscented, but you could colour match to your theme. Or use classic white.

Music

Music can be a great addition to a meal, especially when you've chosen it so perfectly and play it so quietly no one notices it.

In fact, the music should be very discreet, your guests are here to chat and enjoy a meal, not listen to your favourite records (that's a different kind of party).

Your theme may suggest something appropriate; our Italian theme suggests a tenor opera singer (e.g., Luciano Pavarotti), or someone more recent like Dean Martin (*That's Amore!*).

In general, play something slow and calming early in the evening, but as the time approaches for your guests to leave, you could pick up the pace a little to get them moving.

Party Favours

Some "authorities" suggest preparing little goody bags to give your guests as they leave, but I don't think a small dinner party at home is in the order of significance that requires a token of thanks that events like weddings do.

Or the kind of trinket you might offer for a child's birthday party.

I also feel that as I've already spent $35 - $70 per person on food and drink, plus the time and effort I put into the meal, plus the very great joy of my exceptional company, a little gift as well is over the top.

With my cultural background, I expect my guests to be bringing me the party favours! (*See Appendix A: Notes for Dinner Guests*).

SUMMARY

As well as food and drink, you also to consider the practicalities of producing the meal:
- Furniture.
- Cookware.
- Serving ware.
- Crockery, cutlery and glassware.
- Guest soap and clean towels.

And for creating a cosy, theme-based evening:
- Table linens and dressings.
- Music.
- But not party favours.

PART TWO:
Prepare For Your Dinner Party

THIS PART ADVISES YOU ON what tasks you need to do, and when, so when you get to the day of your Dinner Party, all the hard stuff has been done.

CHAPTER 7

3 - 4 Weeks Before

Now we've arrived at the preparation phase. Hopefully, you've read Part One: Plan Your Dinner Party, and are now ready to do it - as Alan Lakein said: "failing to plan is planning to fail".

Clearly, you've the idea that you want to invite some people over for dinner, or you'd not have bought my book (thanks again!).

Perhaps you've done something about it, or maybe you're still in the research phase. In either case, it's time to get practical and get started.

Or as we Project Managers like to say, execute the plan.

You'd probably like to do the full *Downton Abbey* experience, but if you're not an accomplished host I strongly advise you to host one or two simple meals before levelling up.

That kind of "proper" dinner requires more sophisticated planning and management than one person can easily carry off as their first attempt.

If you'd like this sort of experience for your guests, a better way is to work with an upmarket hotel for a private party in a small function room.

This kind of event is surprisingly inexpensive as you can order food and drinks menus at different price points, and these packages include the room hire and service staff, and in some cases a free or heavily discounted bedroom.

Or if that sounds too grand, ask a caterer what sort of packages they can offer. Some firms will deliver cold food for you to heat up, others will cook, serve and clean up in your home.

In the meantime, I'm assuming you'll cook and serve a simple affair at home. Once you've completed one or two small Dinner Parties, you'll have a better idea of how to scale up for larger groups or to develop more formal occasions.

I call it a simple affair, but even simple affairs aren't really simple. In fact, simple things are often the most difficult.

That's why this book is not called *Dinner Parties for Dummies*.

That and the copyright thing.

All things considered, you can't go far wrong with fresh seasonal ingredients prepared to maximises their flavour.

But back to business.

The Very First Thing

Start a notebook or file to keep all your Dinner Party details in. It can be paper, a computer file, Evernote notebook or any other thing that works for you. As I mentioned in Chapter One: Budget, write down your objective:

> Host an Italian Themed Dinner Party for six people for $500 on October 4.

If you know who your guests are you could include their names in the objective, then note what you know about your guest's dietary requirements.

Include copies of your recipes, and as your plans flesh out write EVERYTHING down in your Dinner Party Book - don't trust yourself to remember the details.

If you get into this habit, everything you need to know is all in one place and you know where that is. Right down to why you chose carrots over broccoli, it's all there.

Include a Master shopping list with everything from the extra teaspoons to fresh parsley to dried pasta.

Buy as much of it over time as you can so when you get to the day, all you need to buy is the ingredients that need to be very fresh.

Every time you think of something, add it to the list - lilac scented hand soap? On the list.

As you host more dinners and parties, you'll find that you draw against these records for your planning. And as your expertise grows, you'll develop your own way of organising the information so that it's readily available when you need it.

In the Halcyon Days, hostesses would keep detailed records in books or on index cards categorising their guests in various ways, for example, card players, young men who dance, witty talkers, and even good friends who can be invited at the last minute to make up the numbers.

I know it sounds snobby, but even my Etiquette Heroines recommend guest logs with information describing A and B list dinner guests, not to mention the Z list that you just can't dodge for some reason.

Naturally you need to code it, so if it's found, people won't be able to guess which list they're on. And you might like to know that my Etiquette Heroines recognised the need to "un-friend" people, though they described it as deleting them from their guests lists.

Your Dinner Party Book will join this long tradition of Books containing details of meals and guests for future references. Then next time "Kyle" comes over you'll know not to include Brussels sprouts on the menu. And you might note that "Tara" turns out to be a terrible bore (Z list), but that "Jenna" is a charming dinner companion (A list).

In the decades to come, you'll enjoy rereading your Dinner Party Book and reminiscing about days gone by, and amusing your children and grandchildren with the old-fashioned ways you did things back then.

We'll be coming back to your Dinner Party Book later.

Pick Your Date

Setting the date is sometimes the hardest part of all, particularly when you're dealing with more than one group of guests.

Katy has such an active social calendar I need to book three months in advance to get her. However, Toseland is much more easy going and he's almost always ready to attend at a moment's notice (though I sometimes wonder whether he stands people up to come to my dinners).

It's usually best to set your date before you do anything else, and then see if the people you want are available. This works best with a month or two notice, but if you really want your Katy there, you should organise around her availability.

You could also do a quick availability check with your other guests and then send more formal invitations later. Emails from a diary app make it easy to track acceptances and cancellations, but a hard copy by post is much more exciting and provides something concrete as a reminder.

Dates like birthdays are fixed and generally easy to schedule within a month or so, but larger events like Christmas should be planned well ahead because some people will be booked from Thanksgiving very early in the New Year.

If you leave your invitations too late, you risk your guests being unavailable. If you give too much notice, some may forget to arrive if you don't reconfirm closer to the day, or choose to attend someone else's function instead.

It's likely that someone will cancel close to the date of your dinner because they're ill or in some kind of situation that requires their urgent attention.

You could invite substitutes to take their place, but sometimes your first guests will become available again because their circumstances change once more.

You could also invite extras just in case, but you'll have to make all the arrangements for the larger number of guests just in case they're all available which might be a waste. Like when you reach that point of the year when you don't ever want to see another piece of turkey.

Guests

Contact your guests and get them booked in.

You don't need to tell them all the details of your plans, but if you give them an overview, it will help them plan what to wear accordingly.

Naturally, if you hope for *The Great Gatsby*, you don't want *London Punk* turning up on the night.

Update your Dinner Party Book with any information such as dietary requirements you need to remember.

Theme

If you haven't already, decide your theme (write it in your Dinner Party Book).

Food

This is the time to start buying your supplies, particularly if you've a young pantry that's not necessarily well endowed with herbs, spices and preserves.

This is also useful as some ingredients may be difficult to obtain, particularly if you're not within easy reach of the kind of large store that stocks exotic ingredients like rose water, tarragon vinegar or truffle oil.

You may need to change your menu or do an internet search for substitutes if you can't get what you need, and the more time you have for this, the better.

Just add one or two speciality items to your usual shop so you don't face a single massive bill for the dinner.

At this stage, your plans are still fluid, so you should start trialling your dishes.

This is partly so you'll be comfortable with the process, and partly to give you an idea of how long the dishes will, in fact, take to make.

It once took me more than 90 minutes to make a Jamie Oliver 30-minute meal, so I can't emphasise this point enough. (Worth the wait, and way quicker the next time).

Knowing what to expect is a fundamental part of feeling in control of the event.

These practice runs will also give you ideas about where you can save time, effort, and money, and perhaps crockery and serving ware as well.

Most recipes also assume a certain level of basic knowledge, such as soaking anchovies in milk to draw the salt out, or salting eggplant to draw out the bitterness.

It's much better to discover you lack this sort of knowledge before your guests do.

You might also find your recipe does not use as much garlic or chilli as you and your guests prefer so you might want to add more (or less if the reverse).

Or even worse, that there's been a misprint and you can't reason out what you're supposed to do with the ginger.

Another useful point to note is that you can swap fresh and dried herbs, but you need to more fresh than dried as the drying process intensifies the flavour. Twice the amount is usually a good first trial, but again, you can adjust this to suit your taste.

Some recipes give you make ahead notes, and these help you put in the least possible effort on the day.

There's nothing worse than madly cooking just within earshot of your guests having a wonderful time.

If you plan to use the make ahead tips on the day, make your trial run with them, to see whether you're satisfied with the way the dish reheats.

Regardless of how and what you do, make your notes directly into the recipes in your Dinner Party Book.

Additionally, if you wanted to up the ante with your own flavoured oil or butter, this is the time to make it.

Drinks

Buying alcohol in bulk can produce savings, so you should start saving towards that. If you don't have an established drinks cabinet to draw against, start buying the spirits and liqueurs you want to serve as you won't be buying these in bulk.

With several wines to drink over the course of the evening, you could choose just one or two *Digestifs* and buy the best you can afford at the time.

Other Needs

Your shopping list is already underway, but don't forget to add your tablecloth, napkins and so on to make sure everything is covered.

Arrangements for Children

Dinner Parties are not the place for children, they're events where adults can mix with other adults in fancy frocks and sparkly jewels.

Often the conversation will be ribald and risqué and most parents prefer their children not be around for that.

There are other dinners and parties that children can and should be involved in, just not "Dinner Parties".

If you can, send them away for the night - perhaps their grandparents or a sleepover with friends.

If you can't send them out, arrange a babysitter or start the meal later when they're (hopefully) asleep.

If you're happy to share your sitter, consider whether you'll provide snacks for the additional children as well, or whether their parents should take care of that.

Your sitter may charge extra for more children so think about whether you want the other parents to help pay.

Whatever you decide, make sure your guests are aware of your decision, and any expectations you're placing on them about snacks and costs.

Arrangements for Pets

Sadly, some people are allergic to pets, and others are just afraid of them.

If you've pets, put some thought into what you might do with them. Especially if they're the sort that will get very excited and jumpy and noisy.

If your pets have particular pieces of furniture that are generally regarded as theirs, there may be some territorial behaviour (as well as a requirement for hardcore cleaning).

You don't necessarily need to board them for the night, you could just contain them somewhere they're not likely to be disturbed by your guests.

If they're not excitable, and your guests are fine with them, you might be able to just leave them doing their usual thing.

Summary

Get a note book to record all your notes and arrangements.
- Cook a trial run and adjust your recipes.
- Keep your comprehensive shopping list up to date.

- Make arrangements for children and pets.

CHAPTER 8

1 - 2 Weeks Before

NOW WE'RE GETTING CLOSER, THIS is so exciting! Take a moment to take a deep breath and savour the feeling.

Every Dinner Party is different, and while the lessons from this one will inform your next, there will never be another moment quite like this.

GUESTS

Follow up with your guests to make sure they're still planning to attend. I wish I could reassure you that this is not a necessary step, but I'm sorry to say that some of your guests will be less excited by your Dinner Party than you are, and therefore less committed to being there.

But at least having confirmed the relevant dates and times with them, you'll know you've done everything you can to ensure they arrive.

If you're inclined, leave them a voice message saying that if you don't hear back by a certain date, you'll assume they're not coming. This provides an easy out for them, and a cut-off for stressing about attendance for you.

And possibly the opportunity to reduce your friendship group to those who want to be with you.

FOOD

By now you should have prepared most if not all of your dishes, and have made any required recipe or menu tweaks. Replenish the supplies that don't need to be fresh.

Around about, this time, try a scaled down practice run of the entire meal. This will give you a better idea of the timing and confirm the dishes can be made at the same time and be served at your scheduled times.

Let's look again at our Italian sample menu:

Apéritif: ricotta and anchovy crostini with Prosecco, optional Campari

Appetiser: penne with roasted pepper sauce and Prosecco

Main: pan roasted veal and green bean salad with Pinot Grigio

Dessert: mangoes and strawberries in sweet white wine with Moscato

Digestif: coffee (or tea), amaretto and biscotti

When you come to finishing and serving the appetiser, you could have the veal cooking, and the pepper sauce laid aside.

You'll require a large pot for the pasta and a small one to melt butter in, and you'll need three suitably sized hotplates or gas burners.

If you can't accommodate this, you'll need to reconsider the menu.

For this menu, you could make the veal earlier and reheat it, or cook it in a slow cooker or the oven or melt the butter in a microwave and adjust your timings accordingly.

DRINKS

Keep stocking up on your beverages and bottled water.

OTHER NEEDS

After your trial cooks, you might find that some of your cookware or serving ware are not as serviceable as you'd hoped. You could go back and use some of the Christmas themed ones you've been given which would be particularly fun if you can tie each ugly piece to one of your guests.

Or you might prefer to borrow or replace them.

Prepare Your Home

With the food under control, now's the time to focus on your home. I know I say now, (two weeks out) but if you've a lot to do, feel free to start earlier.

Katy and I both use Dinner Parties as excuses for really deep housecleaning.

All my Etiquette Heroines suggest a neat and clean house (attended by thoughtful and well-groomed staff) is an indicator of good breeding and reflects the spirit of its owner.

I do wish I was more dedicated and more house proud, but in my opinion, there are way better things to do with my time.

If you're not like me, and your house is immaculate, make yourself a cup of tea and put your feet up. You deserve it!

But if you're like me, it's time to roll your sleeves up and focus on DEEP cleaning. Grab your Dinner Party Book, and get ready to write a list of all the things that need to be done for the party.

Go outside, stand on the road and look at your house. If you don't own the street frontage, stand in the corridor of your apartment building instead.

You may not be able to do much more with these public areas than ask the building manager to arrange cleaning and maintenance.

If you're community minded, you could invite your neighbours to help you clean and mend for beer and snacks, or do as much or as little as you need to spruce up the appearance.

If you want to put out decorations, go ahead if your rules permit this and you're confident they'll still be there in the morning.

Looking at your house, unit, apartment or whatever, make a note of general unattractiveness.

Stress Free Dinner Parties

Is there weeding that needs to be done? Where can you put your garbage cans so they aren't the first thing your guests see or smell? Write it on your to-do list in your Dinner Party Book.

Walk towards your front door. Do you need some additional light to help your guests navigate through the jungle to the door, or should you do some pruning?

You don't have to renovate the whole garden, just a little tidy up to make it easy for them to get to the house without damaging their clothes. On the list.

Ring the doorbell to make sure it works.

While you're there, should you sweep the porch and wash the windows?

Are there any big cobwebs that need removing?

Would a little pot plant by the step make the property look more inviting?

If you're planning to send smokers out here, is there a pot for the butts, and do you have seats for them? (The list).

Stand at your front door and look into your home:

- Do you see any piles of things like newspapers or charity/thrift store drop offs that need to be moved?

- Where will you put your guests' coats? Do you have a rack? Do you have the space to put one nearby? Or will you need to lay them on a bed in the next room?

- Is the hallway festooned with cobwebs? Are there leftover decorations from seasons gone by? I hope as I mention these things, and as you stand there looking, I don't need to tell you to put them on the list to remove them.

Walk through your home and imagine yourself taking coats, and pointing out where the bathroom is, offering and making *apéritifs* and inviting your guests to sit down.

Ask yourself whether your blender is accidentally doing double duty making cocktails in the sitting room and pureeing soup in the kitchen.

Really notice what the spaces look like and what you can do to improve them.

You're still a couple of weeks out, so weather permitting, you can still hire a carpet cleaner and give the place a quick once-over.

Or you might want to get a floor rug to cover the worst of the wear and staining on the carpet.

Or vacuum the curtains.

And so on.

While you're pretending to offer drinks, look at the seating arrangement. Your furniture is probably circling the television - wouldn't it be much nicer if your guests could sit in small groups looking at each other, with a small table handy to rest their drinks on?

And of course, you'll need somewhere within easy reach for the little nibbles as well.

I recommend you schedule a time to move the furniture around until you're happy with it.

Once I helped a friend get organised on the day of her party, and when we moved the sofa, we found a family of mice living inside it!

While you're at it, why not vacuum underneath it, and in all its nooks and crannies as well so that there will be less dust when you do it for real.

Plan to put away your embarrassing books and recordings, and throw out all the rubbish you find.

Carefully wrap and pack away priceless family heirlooms and other precious things that you don't want to see in pieces at the end of the night.

Stress Free Dinner Parties

Consider whether there are any other things you can put away so that the rooms are seemingly "light and airy", clear and uncluttered.

If like me, you prefer a life with minimal dusting, you may be able to postpone the unpacking for so long no one remembers why you had all that stuff in the first place.

If you're not in an open plan house, do the same for all the areas your guests might reasonably expect to be in.

If you're keen (or a bit paranoid), do the same for the adjacent areas you wouldn't reasonably expect them in as well.

My utility room is wedged in between my dining and lounge rooms so I always feel compelled to at least clear the countertops and shove stuff in the cupboards. Sometimes I even put my clean clothes away.

Have you ever been in a restaurant bathroom that was so filthy you wondered whether you should stop by the Emergency Department on your way home to have your stomach pumped?

Or do you usually find them light, bright and clean suggesting that the kitchen is also maintained to the highest food hygiene standards?

Now look at your bathroom – does this change how you feel about the food coming out of your kitchen?

If you live in an old building and have 100-year-old cracked and stained tiles, your options are limited for deep bathroom cleans (though if you believe the television shopping network, steamers are perfect for that).

However, if there are plumbing issues that need fixing, now's the time to get them done.

While you're in the vicinity, consider whether you want or need to get some new soaps and towels for the night.

Maybe a bowl of flowers or glass pebbles or some other pretty thing. Think about the things that you like to see and smell in hotel and restaurant facilities.

Where can you spare toilet paper rolls that looks nice, but is easy for your guests to get at without asking you for them?

If you routinely use the room for drying clothes, make a note to put them away before people arrive.

Take a look in the cupboards; your guests probably will.

You might like to make sure that your more embarrassing medications and lotions are hidden away. Throw out the nasty old tubes of toothpaste, mostly empty containers of junk, and expired products.

Can you organise what's left in a way that's pretty, functional, and amazes snoopers?

If you want to up the ante, clean the shelves and drawers and put everything back neatly.

Make sure you check the kitchen too.

We aren't always as conscious of hygienic food handling as we like to think we are so you might want to note that the appliance exteriors need cleaning.

Just discard any expired and spoiled food when you see it.

If you do go as far as cleaning the oven, allow plenty of time to cook off the chemical residue before the party.

You might also want to think about where you can accommodate guests who may have drunk too much to drive home.

Prepare Your Yard

If you hope to hold your party outdoors, look at the area and decide how much work you need to do.

Can you just clean and tidy the area or do you need to mend paving or replace decking? Will you need some kind of shade?

Will you need to give your guests maps, pith helmets and machetes to get to the rendezvous location?

How much time and money have you got to get the place up to standard without a reality television show intervention?

Start putting these things and others like mosquito repellent in your Dinner Party Book.

At least hose down your eating area to remove dirt and guano. Scrub your outdoor furniture and leave to dry.

Move tools and all those household project offcuts back into storage (or the bin).

Discard broken or disused furniture as well as dead pot plants and arrange your surviving plants attractively.

Organise your smoking areas, and place your bug repellents in places where they can discreetly do their jobs.

Other Tasks

You might like to make plans for a quick and easy dinner the day after the party.

Prepare a Seating Plan

You could make a seating plan, and write out seating cards. This can be helpful when managing relationships in circumstances where you've no choice, for example entertaining your father, his current and three ex-wives. (Assuming that no one rearranges the cards for fun).

It can also be useful for ensuring special diets make their destinations and considering how you plan to introduce "Cameron's" latest girlfriend to the group.

It can also look pretty, but ordinarily not necessary for a small dinner.

In the Halcyon Days, the host and hostess sat at the ends of the table, with the oldest or most important woman on the host's right, and oldest/most important man on the hostess's left. You might prefer to sit in the middle because it's near the kitchen door, and seat grandpa somewhere draught free.

Men and women were seated alternately with couples split apart. If you can, seat people you know share interests together, and try to keep politically opposed people at opposite ends (unless that's part of your extremist-baiting entertainment plan).

Catch Up with the News

It's your job to keep the conversation moving during service, so you might want to start keeping up with current affairs, sports results and the weather if you don't already.

If you all belong to a local group or church, you can discuss something relevant from there.

If it's the right kind of party, you could have the guests swap seats as the night progresses.

Prioritise Your To-dos

By now you'll have a long list of things to do and buy. Your priorities will be different depending on whether you'll be eating inside or outside so you need to rank the tasks accordingly and get moving on them.

You could do this by the cost, time, or effort required, for example, start by redoing the paving.

Other times a logical plan of approach will suggest itself, such as vacuuming before steam cleaning the carpet.

Or beginning with the most expensive (e.g. furniture) or most urgent (e.g. plumbing).

Plan Your Party Schedule

As your menu firms, you can start planning your dinner schedule. A course will generally take 15 - 30 minutes to eat, followed by a 15 - 30-minute break.

If we start with our basic menu and the knowledge we've invited guests to arrive 6:30 for 7:00, the basic schedule could look like this:

  6:30 drink and snack on arrival

  7:00 first course at table

  8:00 second larger or main course

  9:00 dessert course

  10:00 cheese if you're having it, or retire from the table with coffee and treats

  11:00 start encouraging people to leave

If you prefer to eat later, say 8:00, then you need to reconsider your schedule. Will you allow a longer period for arrivals and perhaps plan a more substantial appetiser? Will you work to a 45-minute course instead of 60 minutes? Or will you continue with the 60-minute course and finish later?

This is all personal preference, be it yours or your guests. If you've a mix of older and younger guests, you might like to have a quicker service so your older guests can leave earlier, and offer a snack later in the evening for the young ones.

You can then take your service times and work back to determine your preparation schedule.

SUMMARY

With 1 – 2 weeks to go, you've already got a good idea of who's coming, and what you'll beating and drinking. Now's the time

to start getting your house, garden and head ready for the party:
- Give the house a deep clean, and work out how you're going to manage the logistics.
- Give your garden a tidy up, and do what you need to do to make it safe.
- Start planning out your Dinner Party schedule.

CHAPTER 9

The Day Before

ALMOST THERE! YOU SHOULD HAVE almost everything under control at this point.

Tomorrow is going to be a very long day. You're going to get up early, work hard, and be awake until the early hours.

Today's about doing everything you can to make tomorrow easy. But first:

RELAX

- You've got a really good idea of who's going to arrive, and even if they don't, at this stage, you can't do anything about it. Take a deep breath and let your shoulders drop. There's no need to think about this anymore.

- You know what your theme is and all the appropriate table decorations, napkins, candles and so on are waiting to be put together. You've got the music. The ambience is in a box (or bag) waiting to be unpacked. Take another deep breath and let your shoulders drop further. You don't need to stress about this.

- You know what your final menu is. You've prepared every single dish and can be reasonably assured that there won't be any food related surprises. Have another deep breath and let your shoulders drop further. It's all going to be okay.

- You know which drinks you're serving. You've bought them all, and they're stacked up ready when you are. Roll your head back and forth across your shoulders and let this concern go.

- The deep cleaning's all done and your home might be cleaner than it's been since you moved in (unless you're a spectacularly clean and tidy person - I know you're out there somewhere). It's all good.

Final Review

You still have some things to do, but you don't have to stress about the big stuff. Get out your Dinner Party Book and look at what still needs to be done and bought.

To-do List

Look through your "to-do" list to make sure there isn't anything critical you've overlooked. If there is, do that first.

If not start with the big, cumbersome and time-consuming work like rearranging the furniture, and deeply cleaning the kitchen and bathroom again.

Shopping List

You'll have to go out early tomorrow to pick up the freshest of the fresh produce, things like fish and flowers that must be in the best possible condition.

Do a quick check just to make sure you do have *all* the supplies you need. You could add milk, tissues and toilet paper to your shopping list, just in case (I'm a bit paranoid about running out of paper goods).

Choose Your Outfit

If you haven't already chosen your outfit, do it NOW!

You don't want to be staring at your clothes rack with nothing to wear and your guests due any minute.

Other Tasks

- Plan a quick, substantial and tasty breakfast.

- Set your alarm for early, and go to sleep knowing that all the big stuff is taken care of.

Summary

You're about ready to go:
- Relax and enjoy knowing you've got this.
- Check your to-do list to make sure you haven't missed anything.
- Check your shopping list to make sure it's under control.
- Choose what to wear.
- Check the weather forecast for meteor strikes!

CHAPTER 10

The Day

Who-hoo! Made it!

There's a lot you need to get done today. Take breaks when you need them, make sure you eat something and drink plenty of water. Especially if you'll be drinking alcohol later.

Morning

When the alarm goes off, GET OUT OF BED!!!

But before you do anything else, sit down, eat some breakfast and savour your morning coffee.

In the fresh air and sunshine if possible, because this will also energise you for the day to come.

Children

Arrange for your parents to pick up the kids this morning. Or if you're letting them sleep over somewhere else, drop them off with a gift as early as convenient for your host family. Preferably on your way to the store.

Shopping

Pack the car with your shopping bags and a cooler to keep your produce cold.

Go out and get all the fresh produce and other things you identified yesterday as necessary. It's tempting to flit around looking at other things, but stay focused and get out of there as quickly as you can.

Don't stop to look at stuff that's not on the list.

Don't buy anything that's not on your list unless you suddenly realise that you don't have enough of something.

Every second you waste outside the house this morning brings you one-second closer to your guests discovering you in your underwear and without your makeup (that's another kind of party).

When you get home, put it all away in the appropriate places while you make yourself a cup of tea or coffee and think about what's next.

Cleaning

You've already taken care of the bulk of this. This is just a touch-up - the gloss on your lipstick if you will.

Go back to the street, and work through the house again to double check on what needs to be done.

Vacuum the floors, put things away and flick a duster about. Spot clean areas you missed or got messed up in the intervening period. Clean the toilet(s) and remove the incriminating evidence from the bathroom cupboards.

If you've more than one bathroom, make sure there are plenty of guest towels and toilet paper available.

If you've just the one bathroom, take care of it on your way out of the shower.

Accept that someone will use your bath towel to dry their hands on unless you move it completely out of their way. This is a perfectly reasonable thing to do if you've somewhere suitable to hang a damp towel to dry in the meantime.

AFTERNOON

Do eat a little lunch if possible. You've been rushing around, and your dinner is still somewhere between five and seven hours away. Try to keep it light as when you do finally eat, it will be several hours of sustained eating.

I'm reasonably sure you won't want to pass on dessert.

Finish the Cleaning

Hopefully, *all* your cleaning is finished now, but if not, make sure that the carpets and toilets are done. If worse comes to worst, these two things will be enough to convince people that you've done the whole house.

Especially if the kitchen looks neatish and organised when they arrive.

Lay the Table

Laying the table is one of those tasks that start with the big things, and then the little things get squeezed into the spaces.

First the tablecloth; ideally ironed flat. Or with the crease perfectly centred down the table.

If you plan to use serving platters, put them on the table so you can work around them.

The the centrepiece (in the centre) and candles.

The candles should generally be new ones, lit as people take their seats. You could cheat and light them as people start arriving, depending on their likelihood of burning the house down and your risk appetite.

Next, covers, other table decorations and condiment sets.

The reason you sometimes see covers being measured out in television shows is so everyone has the same amount of elbow room.

Arrange your place mats, then cutlery, glasses and napkins. Originally, the place mats were plates so if you've enough, feel free to use them instead, but if they have food on them at the end of a course, they must be removed and replaced for food hygiene and safety reasons.

If you plan to plate up your food in the kitchen, you don't need any crockery on the table.

If you'll be using platters and allowing guests to serve themselves, then each person's crockery is stacked up on their mat, with the first to be used on the top.

Except for dessert which is usually brought in after mains, already plated.

For our Italian example, you'd have a small pasta plate on top, and a larger one for the main underneath.

While most restaurants put a bread plate to the left of the cutlery, often with a small (butter) knife across it, bread is not customarily served at Dinner Parties except with a course that requires it or as a garnish.

Cutlery is laid so that whichever pieces are on the outside are the next ones that you use.

For our Italian example: appetiser (pasta fork) on the outside, main (knife and fork) in the middle, and dessert (spoon) on the inside.

When space is tight, you can put the dessert cutlery above the mat or bring it in with desert - have fun with that.

For right handed people, the knife is laid on the right.

Some left handed people eat right handed, and the rest left handed. (I hope that makes sense).

So if you know a guest eats left handed, you could lay their place with the knife on the left.

If you'd like to know all about oyster forks, fish knives and so on, go to a second-hand store and buy an old-fashioned etiquette book.

I've found they're more reliable than online sources, and as a bonus you get handy tips on letter writing and the correct forms of address.

I love this kind of advice, but despite my fondness for oysters, I'm not going to buy a set of cutlery to use once or twice a year.

The only specialty knife I recommend regardless is a steak knife, because you'll probably get a lot of use from it.

The knives are laid with the blade facing the plate. I'm sure there's a deep seated superstition about this, similar to not giving knives as gifts lest they cut the friendship off (which can be mitigated by giving a small payment to the giver) but I don't know what that might be.

In purely practical terms, you don't want your guests to cut themselves and have to spend the evening in the Emergency Department waiting room.

If someone uses the cutlery in a different order, don't stress about it - just discreetly supplement where necessary.

If you hope to hold more Dinner Parties, don't point it out, or make fun of your guest or you'll find your invitations refused.

Glassware is plced above the right-hand cutlery in the same order: appetiser (Champagne) on the outside, then main (wine) in the middle and dessert (small wine) on the inside.

The water glass is always the innermost glass. In our example, we'll be carrying Champagne over from our appetiser so those glasses go in your reception area.

There's no difference between Europe and America, continents in the way the table is laid out.

Americans usually cut things up, then put their cutlery down and pick up their fork in their knife hand to eat, while almost everywhere else uses both implements in opposite hands at the same time.

Different Asian countries have different rules about chopstick use. Generally, it's impolite to point them at people, or rest used sticks on the table, so a set comes with a rest.

The two main variants are on the right side of a cover, "points" (the thin ends) toward the centre of the table. Or below the cover (closer to you than the centre), points toward to the left.

For a Dinner Party with friends at home, it doesn't matter a great deal. If you particularly don't want to offend a guest, go on line and research etiquette for the country your meal is themed aound.

If you're using place cards or have prepared menu cards, they go above the place mat, outside the desert cutlery.

Your basic set of condiments will be salt and pepper though some formal settings also include bottles for oil and vinegar.

Originally guests were given their own salt and pepper as a demonstration of power and wealth, but these days one set alone, or one either side of the centrepiece is usual.

Some cultures have particular condiment requirements, for example at your Chinese themed Dinner Party, you might swap the oil and vinegar for soy and chilli sauces instead.

The last thing I usually do table-wise is to fold my napkins. Artistically fanned or folded creations do look nice, but might also seem a little try hard.

You decide according to whether you think your guests will feel flattered by your effort. I often just fold my napkin in half, and then in thirds to make a rectangle, and slip it under the right-hand side cutlery (which would be more sensible to do before laying the cutlery out).

Napkin folding is one of those things that's easier with practice. Wash and dry your hands before you get started, and carefully inspect each napkin to ensure it's spotless.

Fold them with the minimum of handling and creasing so they maintain their cleanliness and crispness.

You can do this earlier in the day, but if you do, make sure you store them somewhere clean and give them a final check before you place them out.

Meal Preparations

Once the cleaning is done, and the table laid, it's time to start preparing the meal, especially if it's somewhere around 2:00 pm depending on what dishes you're making.

For a 6:30 start, aim to get most of the preparation done by 5:00 so you've time for your personal preparations.

Review your notes and start with the course that requires the most work. Follow the same procedure as your rehearsal, remembering to wash the tools you'll need again, and stack the dishwasher as you go.

Once you've finished the first dish, tidy up, wipe down the countertop and start again with the next, and then the next.

Personal Preparations

Once you've finished your food prep, take a shower, do your face and get dressed.

Get at least the basics of your make-up on because you don't know if you're going to lose a bit of time due to early arrivals or a misplaced dish towel or similar.

You could leave your heels off, but do wear your hosiery so you can just change your shoes on the way to the door.

Make sure you're wearing your apron. You haven't got this far to have to change at the last minute.

DINNER SERVICE

As your guests arrive, put their coats in the place you prepared, bring them through to your comfortable reception space, offer them a drink and invite them to eat your snacks.

In the Halcyon Days, it was usual to save guest gifts for personal use later.

While some guests will tell you to save it for later, many now expect you to open and serve their gifts as appropriate in the order of service. Up to you on this one.

In those times, polite (on time) society would have to wait until their late dinner companions arrived.

I'm not so polite, mainly because I'm usually the one who's early and circling the block for fifteen minutes waiting for the time to tick over.

I believe it's more or less as high as the height of bad manners can get to be late, particularly as I've already given you a thirty-minute window.

If you're late to any of my functions, I will start without you, and I advise YOU to commence dinner service on time.

If your late guests finally arrive, you can say something like "I was sure you wouldn't want us to wait for you."

You could offer them service from the first course, or do as I do and just start them where you're at.

I'm aware some cultures give you a time frame so you can add an hour or two onto that time, and if that's your custom, go with that.

If this makes you feel bad, consider the feelings of your more timely guests who're now facing a meal presented in less than perfect order.

If you don't start and proceed on schedule, the rest of your food will be served at less than its optimal best, you'll feel stressed, and it will affect everyone's enjoyment.

If your latecomers were thoughtful people, they'd have already told you they were running late and asked you to carry on without them.

And if they haven't contacted you, it's more likely they'll not arrive at all.

When everyone is seated, and the first course served, say a prayer or blessing if this is your practice, or invite them to eat.

Generally, you'd leave the plates on the table until you're ready to serve the next course.

This allows people the maximum time to eat given they'll hopefully be doing a lot of talking as well.

Well brought up people will place their cutlery together on the plate to indicate they've finished eating, but rest the knife and fork on opposite sides if they're still going.

If your hour is nearly up, don't feel embarrassed to ask if they've finished so that you can move on.

I recommend you take the plates out one in each hand at a time just for the sake of quietness. It's fine to accept assistance if someone's thoughtful enough to offer.

Dishes are generally removed from the right and replaced at the left, drinks and knives replaced from the right, and forks from the left.

Coffee service is the first indicator to your guests the evening is coming to a close.

Retiring to a separate reception area allows them to form their own groups and speak with people they haven't got to yet. It also gets them standing and moving, which makes it easier to get them to leave.

In the Halcyon Days, men commonly retired to the smoking room and women (who didn't smoke) retired to the drawing room. But they all gossiped, and after a bit, the men rejoined the women. A tradition that continued even after women started smoking.

Modern homes don't generally have enough spaces for such segregation, though you may see a mass exodus of smokers at this point so it's kind of the same thing.

Most will drink their coffee, then offer to help you clean up, and when you refuse they'll leave. Usually, once the first one departs, the rest will follow fairly shortly after.

AFTER DINNER

It's up to you whether you accept offers of assistance or not.

These days with a functioning dishwasher, clean-up is quick and easy, but if your dishwasher isn't electric and plumbed in (i.e. a person), then take the help that's offered!

Stress Free Dinner Parties

In any case, you need to do it and the noise of cleaning up often triggers the exodus of your more leisurely guests.

However, you may need to start yawning widely, ostentatiously looking at your watch (if you don't have one, it's well worth buying one for this use alone) or chatting about picking the kids up in the morning.

It's possible you'll need to say something like "Thank you so much for coming" or even go a little further and say something like "I'm so sorry, I'm utterly exhausted, and you really must leave now".

Only probably nicer because you're not me!

You might be left with someone who's drunk too much to be safe on the road, so you can either call them a taxi or permit them to sleep over if you've made provision for this.

Once you've cleared the house, give yourself an easy start for the morning:

- Finish stacking the dishwasher to its full capacity and turn it on.

- Put any food you want to keep in containers in the refrigerator.

- Put some hot water and dish soap in your very dirty dishes like roasting pans.

- If your linens are stained, put them in to soak. I use a sodium percarbonate and enzyme nappy (diaper) washing powder - it's excellent for red wine, blood and fat. Almost any organic stain. I'm told dishwasher detergent, or washing soda are good substitutes but I haven't tried them myself.

- If you've permitted smoking in your home, put the ashtrays outside so the aroma is not trapped in the house.

- Open a couple of windows a little to air the place out overnight.

- Wipe down the countertops.

- Get the coffee pot ready to go so that all you have to do in the morning is flick the switch.

Summary

It's the big day!
- Start by getting up early and eating breakfast.
- Spend the morning shopping and finish the cleaning.
- In the afternoon, prepare the table, get the cooking underway, and get dressed.
- Enjoy your meal!
- Do a little cleaning up before bed.

CHAPTER 11

The Day After

Whew! You made it. I hope you had a great time and want to do it all over again. Even if it's not anytime soon!

First things first. Push the start button on the coffee maker!

While you're waiting, open all your curtains and weather permitting, throw open all the doors and windows and get some fresh air in.

Empty the dishwasher and scrub any remaining dishes. If you're ready, put your linens in the clothes washer to rinse.

Take your coffee outside, breathe in the fresh air and appreciate the stillness (and hopefully quietness).

Eat a hearty breakfast to set yourself up for the day. Even though it means you'll have to do the dishes again.

Move your furniture back to its usual places, unpack your precious things (if you like), return them to their homes and bring your house back into living mode.

Go get the kids and maybe do something fun as a family on the way home.

Write thank you notes to return with any dishes you borrowed.

Allow yourself to smile at odd times as you remember things that happened at dinner.

When you're ready, update your Dinner Party Book with food and friend information you didn't previously know.

Write some notes on how the menu went, and your opinion about whether you might use some or all of it again.

You could also transfer your recipe notes back to the original source for future reference.

Summary

- Air out your house and finish your clean up.
- Do something fun with your family.
- Update your Dinner Party Notebook.

APPENDIX A: Notes for Dinner Guests

AREN'T YOU LUCKY? SOMEONE LIKES you enough to invite you into their home so they can share their food with you.

They hope you'll enjoy a delicious meal, some fine wine and scintillating conversation. They want to make you happy.

You might be the best of friends. You might have known each other your whole lives. But there are still limits to what you can and can't do when you're invited to a Dinner Party.

A Dinner Party is a special event. It's nothing like when you call past one evening and they ask you to stay to eat.

You're expected to dress up and put your company manners on. And as a good guest, it's your responsibility to be witty and entertaining.

It doesn't matter what else is going on in your life, for those few hours, nothing else matters but the people at the table.

It's like going out to dinner at a classy restaurant, except that the restaurant is someone's home.

And the food might not be quite as classy, but restaurant chefs don't deliver your food to the table and then sit down and chat with you.

Restaurant chefs only care about you so far as you can pay the bill, and they can pay their staff, buy supplies and put a little something in the bank.

Your Dinner Party host has thought about what they can do to please YOU.

They've considered what you might like to eat and drink. They've thought of your comfort and laid out fresh soap and clean towels.

Maybe the first time they cleaned the toilet was when you said you'd come for dinner. They've stocked up on supplies they wouldn't usually eat - there's probably a $20 bottle of fancy oil that won't ever be finished in the pantry now because you said you'd come.

That's an awful lot of time, money and effort consciously expended just for YOU.

Do you see where I am going with this?

RSVP

From the French "*Répondez s'il vous plaît*", meaning "Reply if you please". Make sure you accept or decline quickly - don't leave your host on tenterhooks wondering whether you'll be there or not.

And don't accept invitations if you don't want to attend.

If you've a medical condition that requires dietary adjustments such as diabetes, food allergies or intolerances, tell your host and offer suggestions about managing them.

If you're a vegetarian as a result of a strong moral choice, you might like to lightly mention your boundaries (e.g. diary but not fish). However, if you're not prepared to make any exceptions, either don't accept or be willing to eat what you can from what's offered.

If you're following a lifestyle diet (e.g. paleo, cabbage soup, Atkins, etc.) then just don't mention it and take a night off - it won't kill you.

Don't bring a friend if your host has not invited you to. If your partner is invited, let your host know if they can't attend or changes entirely between getting your invitation and your arrival for dinner.

Dress Appropriately

Dinner Parties are usually adult affairs, with food that's a little fancier than usual, so the dress is a little fancier too.

Do make the effort to bathe and put on some nice clean clothes for dinner.

Your host will have given you an idea of the style of dress they expect, so if they have asked for cocktail dress don't wear jeans. For a little guidance see below.

The theme generally indicates what the expectations are. "Titanic" suggests formal evening wear, "Christian's [first adult] Birthday" suggests semi-formal and "Christian's [last childhood] Birthday" will most likely be casual.

The "Italian" menu used in this book could go either way. It feels informal, so if your host would like you to dress more formally, they'll tell you what level of dress they expect.

Below are some styles of dress. The most formal and codified is the white tie, with relaxing expectations and greater freedom of expression as you work your way down to casual.

White Tie

The most formal of Western dress and now generally only worn after 6:00 pm at *very* formal events like State Dinners. It comes with specifications about what *must* be worn. As a cheat, think Fred Astaire and Ginger Rogers, but should you ever be invited to a proper white tie event, make sure you do your homework.

Black Tie

Also known as morning dress, this is a slightly less formal dress than white tie, again worn after 6:00 pm. For men a dinner suit (tuxedo), white shirt and black bow tie, and for women full-length ball gowns, best jewellery and heels. This is perfect for the "Titanic" theme.

Cocktail

A semi-formal sort of transition from day to night attire. It arose from the inter-war period when it became common to meet for drinks before dinner. It's less regulated than "tie" codes, but men should wear a dark dress suit (not tuxedo), white shirt and tie. Women should wear a black, white or jewel-toned short dress in a luxurious fabric (with or without beading or metallic effects) bold jewellery and heels. More recently some women prefer to wear a tuxedo. This one works for "Murder on the Orient Express", and coming of age parties.

Lounge Suit

A little more relaxed than the cocktail dress code. For men a neutral suit (e.g. grey or navy) with a tie. For women, knee-length dresses, simple jewellery and heels. This would work for "Italian", but your host will guide you on their expectations.

Smart Casual

More relaxed than lounge. For men, pants and blazer with a collared shirt, but not necessarily a tie. For women, separates are acceptable. NO JEANS ALLOWED!!! This dress code would also be good for our "Italian" theme.

Casual

Neat and clean, jeans and sneakers. Whatever! Probably most appropriate for last childhood events.

ARRIVE ON TIME

Plan your trip to ensure you'll arrive sometime within the window given (e.g. 6:30 pm for 7:00), at the very latest by the time the meal is to be served (7:00). Under no circumstances should you arrive early. If you arrive early, your host may still be making their preparations, or possibly in a state of undress.

If something delays you, telephone as soon as you know you're going to be late. *Speak* to them and tell them when you expect to arrive.

Tell them not to hold the meal up for you because you want them to enjoy the meal as it was intended to be eaten - not overcooked and dry because you were delayed. DO NOT TEXT - you need to be sure they've received your message.

When you arrive, they may offer you the first course, but to make it easier for them, say you'll just start where they are.

Don't change your mind at the last minute and just not turn up. Once you've accepted, the only thing that should prevent you from being there is death.

Or a near death emergency.

And in the remote circumstance that one does come up, do the decent thing and telephone to speak to them. Tell them you were looking forward to being there, and are devastated that you've been prevented.

You hope that you can make it up to them in a few days or weeks when this emergency is over.

It's best if you can speak to them, but sometimes life's not like that and you might have to text or leave a message, but this should be your fall-back position, not your starting point.

The very least that you can do is to turn up because you said you would. In fact, you kind of promised. And if you don't arrive, you may find that your access to and intimacy with your host is restricted.

TAKE A GIFT

It's not only traditional to bring a small gift for the host, but it's also a nice gesture of thanks for the effort tha's been made on your behalf.

If you ask, they'll usually say that you don't need to bring anything. Don't be fooled, you must take something, but the something is a gift not a component of the meal.

The usual gifts are flowers, a bottle of wine, or some kind of a dessert item like cake or cookies.

These gifts should be planned and well thought out gifts. This is not the circumstance for stopping at a gas station on the way and buying a half-dead bunch of daisies, a cheap bottle of plonk from the sale rack or pre-packaged mass produced cookies from the supermarket.

These things are the kind of thoughtless gifts that drunk people offer when they're afraid they've done something wrong. And if you've ever received one of these gifts, you know that the giver has indeed done something wrong.

If you don't tell your host to save it for themselves (and maybe not even then), they might bring your gift out to show everyone else at dinner. "Look at this charming bunch of flowers "Justin" brought!" Or "Let's try "Morgan's" wine". Maybe even "would anyone like one of "Brandon's" Oreos?"

While I don't want to put a dollar figure on this (because costs vary from place to place) it's possible to buy these tokens relatively cheaply.

I can buy a good sized bunch of fresh flowers from a florist for $15. I could also get a decent bottle of wine or about a pound (450 g) of fresh Italian biscotti. Similarly, if I am hosting a Dinner Party, the cheapest wine I would provide would probably cost about $15 per bottle.

If you examine your own circumstances and consider how much you could spend on a *decent* bottle of wine, this will give you an indication of the minimum you should think about spending on your host gift. Though if you really like them, feel free to spend more.

Alternative gifts could be more personal tokens specific to your relationship with the host. Perhaps in the past, they have admired a piece of art you own and you'd like to give them something by the same artist. Or maybe they commented on some music you were listening to, and you could give them the CD or gift it from the iTunes store.

This is not the time for gift cards.

Do NOT for one moment think that your presence is enough of a gift.

Party Manners

If you don't want your phone to take photos with, turn it off and leave it in your bag. There are only two key activities you need to concentrate on for the next few hours - being a good guest and enjoying the food.

If you haven't already discussed your dietary requirements, don't do it when you arrive - it's too late.

Unlike a restaurant, there's no spare capacity to tailor dishes to your needs. Eat what you can from the food provided, and stop off somewhere on your way home.

Be a Charming Guest

Say please and thank you. Speak with both of your neighbours and the people opposite if you can easily see them.

Allow them to eat as well as talk. Don't sneak out to the toilet to update your social media feeds.

When in doubt about what to talk about, ask someone what they think. People are generally very happy to share their opinions about things. And if someone asks your opinion, leave a space now and again for them to reciprocate.

However, do try to keep to the kinds of topics you'd be happy to discuss over coffee in the morning.

And try not to be so firm about your opinions that you're forever after defined by them - think before you speak and consider the feelings of the person that you're talking to.

If you're seated next to someone you despise, you must still talk to them, partly because it blocks the table when you don't, and partly so you don't distress your host.

Emily Post recounts the story of two dinner guests who politely recited multiplication tables to each other for the sake of their hostess' feelings. Use this as inspiration and follow suit.

In the same vein, it's inevitable that one day you'll have to attend a function where you'll run into someone with whom you've fought and are not on speaking terms.

Don't spend the evening attempting to make them feel awful. Every barb you send at them makes you look horrible and makes the rest of the party very uncomfortable.

Don't be known for the rest of your life as the person who made "Courtney's" Dinner Party so miserable, or "Bradley" so sad he had to leave the state to get away from you.

Just not worth it.

Enjoy the Food

Before eating, it's polite to wait until everyone has been served. In some cases, your host may want to say a prayer or blessing and acknowledge the presence of their Deity, so you should wait for your host to invite you to eat, or start eating themselves.

In the interim, you could say something along the lines of this looks or smells delicious.

Really appreciate the flavours and textures as if it was your last meal ever.

Compliment the chef and discuss the complex interplay of the spices. Even if it's the worst meal you've ever eaten, don't forget that your friend made this food for you so try to find something nice to say.

Don't panic about the cutlery and glassware - start from the outside and work your way in. It's not the end of the universe if you get it wrong - if you run out of cutlery, someone will bring you something to eat with.

If you're very concerned about appearances, do note that gazpacho soup is served cold.

Don't chew with your mouth open; no one ever wants to see that. Not ever.

Try to eat at the same speed as the other guests so your host gets a clear indication of when to introduce the next course.

No Snooping!

You were invited to eat a meal. Eating a meal does not require you to put on a deerstalker hat and snoop through the bathroom cupboards.

You don't need to know what's in them, and you might find your joy in the evening and your host is diminished if you do.

Would you like it if your guests discovered the cream for your foot fungus (or worse)?

Or you haven't bothered to replace your toothpaste yet?

Or you're taking a course of antibiotics for some undisclosed infection?

The mind boggles.

Leave those secrets in the bathroom.

Once you know them, you can't un-know them. Ever.

Can you imagine being friends with this person for the next twenty years knowing their bathroom secrets?

Stand firm and don't open the cupboards.

If you think the toilet paper needs replenishing (etc.) discreetly let your host know.

Smoking

Don't smoke without an invitation to do so.

If no mention has been made, feel free to ask if you can, but don't pout if you're sent outside (the advances of science have established the dangers of passive smoking).

If you're an e-smoker, head outside with the others. And while you're out there, don't talk with your mouth full of cigarette - it makes your face scrunch up and you might look angry or threatening.

Drinking

Keep your drinking under control. It's always better to leave on your own feet than be carried out and poured into the car.

It's also much nicer for your hosts not to have to clean vomit up from all over the house before they can go to bed.

Everyone is different, but in general, two drinks the first hour, and one for each subsequent will keep an average person on the legal side of sobriety. Unless your town has a zero blood alcohol policy.

At the End of the Night

While we sometimes wish it were otherwise, all things come to an end.

Coffee indicates the end of the meal, so 30 - 60 minutes after that, it's time to leave.

You may be having a wonderful time, but do leave within this window as it's always better to leave on a high.

If you're the guest of honour, you should leave as soon as is polite because others may be waiting for you to leave before they go.

Offer to do the Dishes

In the Halcyon Days, you were expected to just say thank you and leave, but knowing your host does not have servants to help them, you should offer to help clean up.

These days most people have dishwashers, so they probably won't accept. But if they do, follow their instructions with good grace and take comfort that after all their hard work, they'll be snoring in their beds before you get home.

And this also places them under the obligation to do the same for you when you return the invitation.

Leave!

If your hosts start clearing away the dishes and wiping down the countertop, it's a good indication they want you to go. As is yawning and commenting about early starts.

So LEAVE!

THE NEXT DAY

Another nice touch is to send a hand-written note or card expressing your appreciation. Or maybe an email, but post with a stamp is nicer. Suggest a date to host them at a dinner of your own.

Apologise

Even with the best of intentions, there are times when we all get a little messy and out of control. Things get broken, or a puddle of something gets left somewhere.

Hopefully, you apologised for your indiscretion on the night. But you must do it again as soon as you're yourself once more. The decent thing to do is to send a token of your sorrow. This may require some research, for example:

- If you broke something, tell them where they can replace it and enclose a gift card for the cost. Or if you want to up the ante, just buy it and send it to them.

- Send wine.

- Send flowers (assuming they're not allergic to them).

- Send some nice chocolates (assuming they're not on a diet).

And then leave it at that. Don't keep on and on at the person you're apologising to.

Be prepared for there to be nothing you can do.

I once basically bullied a friend into using a set of antique wine glasses; an irreplaceable set given to her deceased grandmother as a wedding gift. And then I broke one. The glass could not be repaired or replaced, and neither could the friendship.

APPENDIX B: What Alexandria Does

THESE ARE THE KEY THINGS I do. There are other little suggestions here and there throughout the book.

DATE

I usually pick a date around two months out and don't change it unless my own circumstances prevent me from carrying it out on that day.

I call my guests to see if they're free for dinner and if so, ask them to book me in. If not, I'll chat for a short while and then move onto the next - that way I know with reasonable certainty I'll have the required numbers.

I'm also quite explicit about the time of the invitation. I'll specify something like "6:30 pm for 7:00". This tells my guests they should arrive after 6:30, and we'll eat at 7:00.

GUESTS

Depending on whom I'm inviting I trust them to note the details, or send them an e-invitation to get into their diary (and hopefully let me know if they delete it). Sometimes, for special occasions, I send cards in the mail but not as often as I used to.

FOOD

When I plan to make a recipe I'm not familiar with, I make a half size test run before the event. This helps me to gauge how the dish will fit in the context of the larger meal, and helps me determine quantities for the big day.

I like to prepare all the ingredients so that they're ready to go when I start to cook. I pull everything out of the cupboards and line it up on the countertop. I measure all the ingredients out and complete the chopping, making sure all the ingredients that go into the pot at the same time are held together.

I also clean up as I go, stacking the dishwasher or washing in the sink and leaving things to drain.

My Reliable Menu

My primary focus in hosting dinner is enjoying good company, so I like to keep it simple. Sometimes I go through my recipes and pick things I'd like to make, but usually, I cheat a bit.

Apéritif

I offer dips and *crudités* for my *apéritif*. The main benefit here is that chopping some dipping vegetables doesn't take much additional effort on top of preparing vegetables for the main.

This also helps with the nutritional balance that can sometimes be lacking in luxury dinners.

I commonly offer only Champagne and beer as an *apéritif*. Though Toseland is a gin fiend so if he's coming, I'll ask him to make gin and tonics.

Appetiser

In warm weather, I usually do a plate of antipasto or small salad that can be made ahead and either stored in the refrigerator or placed on the table while we wait for the guests to arrive.

This has the added advantage of being prepared at the same time as the *apéritif* and being ready when the guests arrive. I will usually carry the Champagne through my first course.

My cool weather first courses are generally the kind of soup I can make ahead which has the added benefit of allowing sufficient time for the flavour to improve. If it's onion soup (with gruyere toasties), I'll usually choose a semi-substantial wine like a Beaujolais.

Main

I often roast lamb racks for my main so I can cook the meat and vegetables in the oven at the same time. I'll usually steam some vegetables as well, and use the cooking liquid to make the gravy. There's a winery nearby that makes an excellent Pinot Noir, so I generally default to that.

Dessert

I'll either prepare a fresh fruit based dessert (like the one in the sample menu) or get some kind of cake or tart from one of the excellent local French, Italian or Spanish bakeries.

You may not be so fortunate as to have access to these where you live, but any good traditional baker who uses real milk, eggs and butter will provide excellent cakes and tarts.

Preservation isn't usually an issue as fresh ones don't often leave anything that requires storage.

For the accompanying wine, I prefer a not too sweet Moscato, which coincidentally, is delicious with some cheeses.

Or whatever hasn't been drunk yet - wine doesn't always keep very well.

Cheese

I don't usually cater wines specifically for the cheeses, we just drink what's left and when we run out I start with the *Digestifs*. (I did mention simple and fun didn't I?)

Digestif

For the *Digestif*, I'll offer from my collection of spirits and liqueurs. Almost always port, though I like a Campari. Katy likes whisky with water, and Toseland will take a Jägermeister.

ALEXANDRIA'S OUTFIT

I like to get the bulk of the food cooking and the mess cleaned up before I dress for dinner.

As my social set includes early birds (or at the very least, people who arrive bang on time) I need to shower and make myself presentable with the minimum of time and fuss, yet still allow time for one last sweep to make sure all is in order.

For a more relaxed dinner, I'll wear jeans and a tunic top with low heeled boots and "natural" look makeup. This isn't very different to my usual daytime look, so it signals to my guests that a comfortable and informal evening is on the way.

To up the ante, I wear a semi-fitted silk sheath dress with hosiery and low heels. It's still "natural" makeup, but I'll use less natural colours for example blue eyeshadow instead of pink, and a more glossy lip colour.

When my guests have arrived, and I'm putting on the finishing touches, I wear an apron and take it off when I sit down. I've an open plan kitchen/dining area and this amuses my guests for the 1950s housewife aspect of it.

I NEVER entertain guests in my lounging around the house clothes (anymore). (Katy says this is perfectly acceptable if you've a pyjama theme, and I should chill out).

APPENDIX C: Our Italian Themed Dinner Party

THIS MENU DRAWS AGAINST MARCELLA Hazan's "Sumptuous Summer Dinner" menu from *Essentials of Classic Italian Cooking.*

Menu

Apéritif: ricotta and anchovy crostini with Prosecco, (optional Campari)

Appetiser: penne with roasted pepper sauce and Prosecco

Main: pan roasted veal and green bean salad with Pinot Grigio

Dessert: mangoes and strawberries in sweet white wine with Moscato, Chantilly Cream on the side

Digestif: coffee, amaretto and biscotti

Crostini Bianchi - Ricotta and Anchovy Canapés (for 28 canapés)

The original recipe results in a smooth, salty cheese spread. The anchovy adds a rich savouriness to what's otherwise quite a bland cheese. I don't think it tastes particularly fishy, but you might have a different opinion and that's why I suggest you trial your dishes. If you (or your guests) don't like anchovies, you'll be able to taste them (even if you buy magnificent ones), so you should choose a different canape.

Ingredients
- ½ lb (225 g) fresh ricotta cheese
- 1 tablespoon butter
- 8 anchovy fillets (or to taste)
- 1 tablespoon extra virgin olive oil
- Black pepper

Utensils
- kitchen weigh scales
- measuring spoons
- cheesecloth
- food processor
- cookie sheet/tray
- cutting knife
- spreading knife

Optional
- a squeeze of lemon juice
- grated rind of half a lemon
- 1 tablespoon of chopped parsley

If the cheese is very moist, wrap it in cheesecloth, and hang it to drain for half an hour (or until it stops dripping). Then whizz it and all the other ingredients in a blender until smooth.

Leave it for at least an hour for the flavour to develop.

You can make this as is, but I like to add a little lemon rind and parsley for colour, and flavour. You could also add garlic and chilli, or any other flavours you're fond of.

Smear it on the crostini and serve. You can make your own crostini or use prepared crostini or crackers.

Or you could skip draining the cheese, make it a little runnier and use it as a dip.

Roasted Red and Yellow Pepper Sauce with Garlic and Basil (Serves 4)

You could scale this up for six, but given the total amount of food this menu provides, I'd cook as is to produce a light appetiser. Very fresh peppers give the best results.

Ingredients
- 3 large coloured bell peppers (capsicums)
- 16 - 20 fresh basil leaves
- 2 tablespoons extra virgin olive oil
- 4 peeled garlic cloves
- salt
- 2 tablespoons butter
- ⅔ cup grated parmesan cheese
- 1 lb (450 g) pasta (MH recommends ridged like rigatoni or tubular like penne)

Utensils
- kitchen weigh scales
- measuring spoons
- measuring cups
- grater
- swivel-bladed peeler
- paper towel
- sauté pan
- wooden spoon
- small saucepan
- medium saucepan

Optional
- fresh chilli or flakes

Wash the peppers, cut them open and discard the seeds and core. Peel them with the peeler – this sounds nuts, but works well. It's also a good technique for tomatoes.

If the fruit's really fresh and still a little firm, and you use a light hand, it's easy. Cut into strips about ½" (1.25 cm) wide.

Rinse the basil leaves and pat dry – try not to bruise them as this releases the flavour prematurely.

Smack the garlic with the flat of a knife so it breaks open a little. Heat the oil over medium heat and cook the garlic until it browns lightly, then discard it.

Don't stress too much about this, you're just infusing garlic into the oil to perfume the dish rather than strongly flavour it.

If you think the oil smells garlicky, it's probably enough - better to have cooked the garlic too lightly than to have a sauce that tastes of burned garlic. It's also an excellent way to add a subtle hint of garlic to other dishes – I do it a lot.

There are different ways to deal with the optional chilli; I haven't quantified this because it's a personal taste thing. If you like a hint of chilli, you could fry half a deseeded chilli with the garlic and take it out at the same time.

Or for more intense flavour, deseed and slice it and fry with the peppers; the spiciness will intensify over time.

For freshness, add it as you reheat the sauce. You can use dried chilli, but its heat is intensified by drying.

If you love chilli, you'll already have an idea of how to manage this, but if not, experiment – start with the tiniest amount and work up!

Put the peppers in the pan, and cook for 15 minutes, stirring frequently. They should be soft but still have a little crunch. Salt to taste and remove from the heat.

About 15 minutes before you're ready to serve, cook the pasta according to the packet directions. Common knowledge suggests adding oil to the water to stop the pasta sticking, but this isn't necessary if you're serving immediately.

If you're serving later, for example in a pasta salad, stir the oil into drained pasta.

When you're almost ready to drain and toss the pasta, reheat the peppers and melt the butter over low heat.

Toss the cooked drained pasta with the peppers. Add the butter, parmesan, and basil. Toss thoroughly once more.

Pan-Roasted Veal with Garlic, Rosemary, and White Wine (serves 6)

If you've an objection to veal, you could substitute pork or chicken. But if you've an objection to veal you're probably better to choose a dish designed for a meat you don't object to.

Ingredients
- 3 medium garlic cloves sliced
- 2 lb (900 g) boned veal roast (a single piece)
- a sprig of rosemary OR 1 teaspoon dried rosemary leaves
- 2 tablespoons oil
- 2 tablespoons butter
- Salt and black pepper
- ⅔ cup dry white wine (Pinot Grigio is probably the easiest Italian dry white to get hold of outside of Italy.)

Utensils
- kitchen weigh scales
- measuring spoons
- measuring jug
- sharp, narrow-bladed knife
- oval shaped heavy-bottomed/enamelled cast-iron pot
- wooden spoon
- fork
- cutting boards
- sharp carving knife

If the meat is a flat piece to be rolled up, lay the garlic and rosemary, and some freshly ground pepper on the meat, then roll and tie.

If it's a lump, make a shallow cut and slip a slice of garlic and a few rosemary leaves into the hole; keep going until it's all gone. You can do it randomly or in a pattern – up to you.

Heat the oil and butter over a medium heat and brown the meat. Sprinkle with salt and pepper.

Add the wine and when the bubbles subside scrape the brown meat residue to loosen it into the liquid. Reduce the heat to a simmer and cook for 1½ - 2 hours with the lid ajar.

Turn the meat periodically and if the liquid evaporates add a couple of tablespoons of water.

Or if you've a slow cooker, cook the browned meat and liquid on high for 4 – 5 hours or low for 8 – 12 hours.

Or roast in a covered dish in a preheated oven at 325°F (160°C) for 1¼ - 1½ hours.

When cooked, cut the meat into slices about ¼" (½ cm). Put on a warm plate or platter and sprinkle the cooking juices over the top.

If you're pan roasting you could pre-cook the meat ahead, and reheat in the pan with the juices, or in a preheated oven at 375°F (190°C) for about 10 minutes.

Green Bean Salad (serves 4)

Just a very simple accompaniment: you could use frozen beans, but the best results come from fresh.

Ingredients	Utensils
• 1 lb (450 g) green beans	• kitchen weigh scales
• salt	• measuring spoons
• extra virgin olive oil	• large basin
• freshly squeezed lemon juice (OR red wine vinegar)	• large pot
	• colander
	• tongs or two forks or spoons for tossing

Wash the beans and steam (cook in just enough water to cover) for around 10 minutes. Drain while they're still firm but no longer crunchy.

Put them in a serving bowl, add salt, and toss. Pour over a little oil and a dash of lemon juice or vinegar. Toss and serve.

Mangoes and Strawberries in Sweet White Wine (serves 6)

I find that fresh fruit is generally quite sweet, especially with a sweet wine so I don't usually add sugar. If you don't like mangoes, this is really nice with peaches too.

Ingredients
- 1 large or 2 small ripe mangoes (OR peaches)
- 1½ cups fresh strawberries
- the grated peel of one lemon
- 1 cup sweet white wine such as Moscato (serve with this wine)

Utensils
- fine grater or lemon zester
- measuring spoons
- measuring cups
- knife
- chopping board
- serving bowl

Optional
- sugar to taste

Wash the fruit, remove the strawberry stems and leaves. Cut the big ones into bite-size pieces.

Peel the mangoes (or peaches), and cut the fruit into bite-size pieces. Put them in the serving bowl with the sugar, peel, and wine. Gently toss to combine.

Leave in the refrigerator for 1 – 2 hours, and toss again before serving.

My mother *always* served cream with dessert, and I got used to it that way. I usually make Chantilly Cream, it seems very fancy for such a simple thing - always goes over well.

Shopping List

This list contains all that you need for our Italian menu; you can cross some of it off immediately (e.g., salt and pepper). I'm substituting prepared crostini because there's a lot of preparation for the other dishes. And I love cheese so I'm offering a selection of cheeses as well.

Ingredients

extra virgin olive oil
salt
black pepper
crostini
biscotti
fresh or dried rosemary

butter
parmesan cheese
provolone cheese
taleggio cheese
gorgonzola cheese
fresh ricotta
milk
whipping cream

penne
anchovy fillets

granulated sugar
icing sugar
vanilla paste

coffee
tea

paper (kitchen) towel
toilet paper
nice soap

3 coloured peppers (capsicum)
2 small ripe mangoes
1½ cups strawberries
green beans
fresh basil
7 garlic cloves, peeled
1 lemon

2 lbs (900 g) boned veal

4 bottles Pinot Grigio
4 bottles Moscato
1 bottle of Campari
6 bottles of Prosecco
1 bottle amaretto

Utensils

kitchen weigh scales
food processor
measuring spoons
measuring cups
measuring jug
cheesecloth

chopping knife
spreading knife
sharp, narrow-bladed knife
carving knife
cutting board

grater
lemon zester (if not on grater)
whisk
swivel-bladed peeler
2 wooden spoons
fork
2 tongs or four spoons

sauté pan
small saucepan
medium saucepan
oval heavy-bottomed pot
large pot
cookie sheet/tray

colander

large basin

platter for crostini
serving bowl for dessert
dish for cream
tray for biscotti

milk jug
sugar bowl

6 plates for appetiser
6 plates for main
6 dishes for dessert
6 coffee cups and saucers

6 appetiser forks and spoons
6 knives and forks for mains
6 dessert spoons
6 coffee spoons

6 Champagne glasses
6 wine glasses
6 short tumblers
6 tall glasses

table cloth
bathroom hand towels
table napkins

SCHEDULE

Assuming I've invited my guests to arrive 6.30 for 7.00 pm, the service schedule looks like this:

6:30 pm *Apéritif*: ricotta and anchovy crostini with Prosecco, optional Campari

7:00 Appetiser: penne with roasted pepper sauce and Prosecco at table

8:00 Main: pan roasted veal with green bean salad and Pinot Grigio

9:00 Dessert: mangoes and strawberries in sweet white wine with Moscato

10:00 Cheese: a hard Provolone, soft taleggio, blue gorgonzola and parmesan (you have it on hand so you might as well)

11:00 retire from the table for *Digestif*: coffee, amaretto and biscotti

11:30 start encouraging people to leave

By the time my guests arrive I want to have:

- Crostini plated and on the table with the wine ready to serve.

- A small selection of olives and other preserves ready to go just in case.

- Peppers cooked ready to reheat when the pasta goes on.

- Veal cooked ready to reheat in the oven.

- Beans prepped and ready to cook.

- Fruit and cream prepared in the refrigerator ready to serve.

In fact, I'd like to have all that done by 6:00 so I've time for a sip of wine and a sit-down. And maybe disaster mitigation. But mainly the wine.

So, taking into account the serving times, and the time required to prepare and partially cook the dishes, I can work backwards to come up with a basic preparation schedule.

At a first pass, this results in the requirement to prepare two or more dishes at the same time.

I'm a big fan of doing one thing at a time so I'll adjust the schedule to permit me to focus on one thing at a time.

2:30 *apéritif*: drain ricotta

2:35 main: stuff meat with garlic and rosemary

2:50 main: brown meat

3:05 main: put meat on to cook

3:10 *apéritif*: blend cheese and anchovy

3:15 *apéritif*: leave to develop

3:20 dessert: wash and chop fruit

3:50 dessert: add wine, sugar and lemon and leave to steep

3:55 make Chantilly Cream

4:00 appetiser: wash and chop peppers, wash and dry basil

4:15 appetiser: sauté garlic and cook peppers

4:30 appetiser: turn heat off and put pan aside

4:35: main: prep beans ready to cook

5:00: main: slice meat and put in a casserole dish ready to reheat

5:15: personal: shower and get ready

6:00 open the first Prosecco and have a glass (quality control if you need an excuse)

6:30 guests start arriving

6:45 appetiser: cook pasta and reheat peppers

7:00 appetiser: serve

7:40 side: steam beans

7:45 main: put meat in oven to reheat

7:55 side: dress beans

8:00 main: serve

9:00 dessert: serve

9:45 cheese: put on platter with accompaniments

10:00 cheese: serve

10:45 put coffee on, prepare tray with biscotti, milk, sugar and liqueur glasses

11:00 serve coffee and liqueur

11:30 start encouraging leave-taking

In my early Dinner Party days I'd schedule the whole day (shopping, cleaning, etc.) but now I usually just start my meal preparation around 2:30 and work through until it's complete before preparing myself for the party.

If your Dinner Party is to be held at noon, you can follow the same process but start around 08:00 am.

Or prepare some of your dishes the night before.

Glossary

À la française (French or family style): all dishes are brought to the table at the same time and guests serve themselves.

À la russe (Russian style): dishes are brought to the table in staged courses.

Alcohol Unit: a legislated amount of alcohol that gives you an indication of the strength of your drink. See also Standard Drink.

Apéritif: a small alcoholic beverage served before a meal to stimulate the appetite. Often served on arrival with a small snack.

Appetiser: a small first course served at the table. Some countries refer to this as entrée.

Blood Alcohol Content (BAC): A measure of pure alcohol in the blood, used to indicate the level of intoxication for legal and medical purposes. Also known as Blood Alcohol Concentration.

Condiment: a substance added to food after it's cooked for additional flavour, such as mustard, sauce or preserves like chutney or pickle.

Cover: a set of all the crockery, cutlery and linen required for one person.

Dessert: a small sweet course served at the table.

Digestif: a small alcoholic beverage served after a meal to stimulate digestion. It's usually served with coffee and a little sweet treat.

Entrée: see appetiser.

Halcyon Days: happier and more peaceful times that are now passed. In this book, used to describe the inter-war years.

Main: a second larger course served at the table, usually with side dishes.

Reliable Menu: one that's easy to cook and produces consistent results.

Sides: dishes (usually vegetable) served on the side, as an accompaniment to the main course.

Standard Drink: a given volume of alcohol that contains a legislated concentration of pure alcohol. See also Alcohol Unit.

Bibliography

Beeton, Isabella. Reproduced in facsimile 2000. *The Book of Household Management*. London: Cassell & Co.

Frederick, Christine. 1923. *Household Engineering: Scientific management in the home*. Chicago: American School of Home Economics.

Hazan, Marcella. 1992. *Essentials of Classic Italian Cooking*. New York: Alfred A. Knopf, Inc.

Hillis, Marjorie. 1937. *Orchids on Your Budget: Or live smartly on what have you*. Indianapolis: The Bobbs-Merrill Company.

Martin, Judith. 1979. *Miss Manners Guide to Excruciatingly Correct Behaviour*. Harmondsworth: Penguin Books.

Post, Emily. 1922. *Etiquette in Society, in Business, in Politics and at Home: The timeless, definitive guide to proper manner and conduct*. New York: Funk & Wagnalls Company.

Index

Alcohol Units 50
Ambience 60
  candles 63
  centrepieces 62
  linens 61
  music 63
  party favours 63
  theme 29
Apéritif
  drink matching 40
  serving size 35
  what Alexandria does
  120
Appetiser
  drink matching 41
  serving size 35
  what Alexandria does
  120
Beer
  glasses and pouring ... 49
Blood Alcohol Content .. 52
Budget 9
  drinks 39
  food 31
  other needs 55
  party favours 63
  reduce costs ... 32, 34, 35
Candles 63
Can't Cook 37
Centrepieces 62
Champagne
  glasses and pouring ... 47
Cheese
  drink matching 43
  serving size 36
  what Alexandria does
  121

Children 74
Cooking Utensils 59
Covers 58
Date 71
  what Alexandria does
  119
Dessert
  drink matching 42
  serving size 36
  what Alexandria does
  121
Dessert and Fortified
Wines
  glasses and pouring ... 48
Dietary Requirements
  drinks 40
  food 32
  guests 14
Digestif
  drink matching 43
  serving size 37
  what Alexandria does
  122
Dress Code
  black tie 110
  casual 111
  cocktail .... See
  lounge suit 110
  smart casual 110
  white tie 109
Drinking and Driving 50
Drinks
  alcohol units 50
  blood alcohol content 52
  budget 39
  dietary requirements . 40
  food matching 40

141

fortnight before 79
how much 43
ice............................... 45
month before 74
standard drinks 50
theme........................... 29
water/soft options..... 45
Entrée .... see appetiser
Food............................... 31
budget.......................... 31
dietary requirements 32
fortnight before 78
month before 72
theme........................... 28
what Alexandria does
.... 119
wine matching............ 40
Furniture 57
Glasses and Pouring....... 46
beer.............................. 49
Champagne................. 47
dessert and fortified
wines 48
red wine 48
spirits........................... 49
white wine 47
Guests 13
dietary requirements 14
family........................... 19
fortnight before 78
getting them to turn up
.... 23
matchmaking.............. 22
month before 72
numbers 15
smokers........................ 21
to avoid 17
to include.................... 18
what Alexandria does
.... 119
what to tell them........ 22
who to invite 17
work colleagues 21

Home Comforts............. 60
Ice................................... 45
Just Starting Out 37
Linens 61
Main
drink matching........... 41
serving size 36
what Alexandria does
.... 121
Menu
balance 33
cooking method 34
dietary requirements. 32
number of courses..... 34
reliable......................... 37
seasonality 33
serving sizes 35
Music............................... 63
Notes for Dinner Guests
.... 107
arrive on time...........111
dress appropriately.. 109
party manners 113
RSVP..........................108
take a gift.................. 112
Number of courses......... 34
Other Needs
budget.......................... 55
Outfit
what Alexandria wears
.... 122
yours........................... 29
Pets................................. 75
Place settings ....see covers
Practicalities
cooking utensils 59
covers 58
furniture...................... 57
home comforts........... 60
serving ware 58
Prepare your home 80
Prepare your yard 84
Recipes

chantilly cream 38
crostini 32
crostini bianchi 124
gravy from scratch 20
green bean salad 130
mangoes and
    strawberries in sweet
    white wine 131
marinated olives 32
pan-roasted veal in
    garlic, rosemary, and
    white wine 128
prosciutto wrapped
    melon 37
roasted pepper sauce
    with garlic and basil
    126
salad dressing 38
slow cook meat stew . 37
Record Keeping 69
Red Wine
    glasses and pouring.... 48
Reliable Menu 19, 21, 37
    what Alexandria does
    120
Schedule
    day after 105

day before 89
drinks 74, 79
food 72, 78
fortnight before 77
guests 72, 78
month before 67
prepare your home 80
prepare your yard 84
the day 93
Serving Sizes 35
Serving ware 58
Smokers 21
Spirits
    glasses and pouring.... 49
Standard Drinks 50
Theme 27
    ambience 29
    drinks 29
    food 28
    your outfit 29
What Alexandria Does
    119–22
White Wine
    glasses and pouring.... 47
Who to invite 17
Won't Cook 37

Author's Note

Thanks again for buying my book.
If you'd like to let me know what you think, drop me a line at hello@alexandriablaelock.com and

I've really enjoyed writing it, and I hope it's been useful for you. In fact, I hope it'll continue to serve you for many years to come.

I've a recipe book that I can never throw out because it tells me the time and oven temperatures for roasting meats and I'm continually going back to it to remind myself.

Hopefully this book becomes the same type of reference for you only smaller and not quite so splattered with cooking fat - something that's always handy for checking on serving sizes and glass shapes and that sort of thing.

For some examples of Stress Free Dinner Party menus, visit alexandriablaelock.com/books/stress-free-dinner-parties/or my Pinterest Board for other interesting information at pinterest.com.au/alexblaelock/stress-free-dinner-parties/

For more, visit me at alexandriablaelock.com to:
- read my blog
- sign up for *Letters from my* Library to stay up to date on the development and release of my books. You'll also get research interestingness (that doesn't get to the blog), gossip about my writing life, and the odd special offer.

About the Author

Alexandria Blaelock writes self-help books applying business techniques to personal matters like getting dressed, cleaning house, and feeding your friends.

She also writes short stories, some of them for *Ellery Queen's Mystery Magazine* and *Pulphouse Fiction Magazine*.

As a recovering Project Manager, she's probably too fond of sticking to plan. She lives in a forest because she enjoys birdsong, the scent of gum leaves and the sun on her face.

When not telecommuting to parallel universes from her Melbourne based imagination, she watches K-dramas, talks to animals, and drinks Campari. At the same time.

Discover more at www.alexandriablaelock.com.

www.ingramcontent.com/pod-product-compliance
Lightning Source LLC
Chambersburg PA
CBHW050316010526
44107CB00055B/2261